Burma and Pakistan: A Comparative Study of Development

PRAEGER SPECIAL STUDIES IN
INTERNATIONAL ECONOMICS AND DEVELOPMENT

Burma and Pakistan: A Comparative Study of Development

Mya Maung

Foreword by
E. E. Hagen

PRAEGER PUBLISHERS
New York • Washington • London

The purpose of Praeger Special Studies is to make specialized research in U.S. and international economics and politics available to the academic, business, and government communities. For further information, write to the Special Projects Division, Praeger Publishers, Inc., 111 Fourth Avenue, New York, N.Y. 10003.

PRAEGER PUBLISHERS
111 Fourth Avenue, New York, N.Y. 10003, U.S.A.
5, Cromwell Place, London S.W.7, England

Published in the United States of America in 1971
by Praeger Publishers, Inc.

Library of Congress Catalog Card Number: 70-146816

Printed in the United States of America

FOREWORD

In the mind of the layman, the less developed countries (LDCs) are often an undifferentiated mass. The peoples who compose the mass are distinguished from us Westerners in that they have low income, whereas we have high income; their numbers are growing so rapidly that increase in productivity cannot keep pace with the population growth, and, therefore, their income is not growing, whereas ours is.

Students of economic development know that these generalizations are wrong on all counts. Per capita incomes vary so greatly among both the less developed and the developed countries that the conception that the world is dichotomized into two groups is a myth. Rather, the distribution of income among all of the countries of the world forms a continuum, with the scatter of countries a little thinner in the middle than in the top and bottom thirds, but still a continuum, not a dichotomy.

Population growth rates, though higher on the average in the less developed than in the developed countries, vary greatly among the former. And in spite of the rapid population growth in some lower income countries (or possibly on account of it), since the mid-1950s, in all of those countries taken as a group, per capita income has risen almost as fast as in the developed countries. Indeed, it has risen as fast as the average rate in the United States during the nineteenth and twentieth centuries.

It is a commentary on the relativity of the concept of underdevelopment that, as income has risen, so has the notion of Western scholars of what is a "low" income. Six or eight years ago, the income level of $500 per capita was regarded as the line dividing the LDCs from their more fortunate contemporaries. Today, an income level of $600 is used. Some countries are classed as less developed only because they passed the $500 level a few years too late. The growth rate comparison would be even more favorable to the LDCs except for the fact that the most rapidly growing of them have burst through the arbitrary ceiling we place on underdevelopment, even while we have been raising that ceiling. Japan and Israel are current examples. Eliminating their remarkably fast growth rates

v

from the average for the less developed group lowers, of course, the average for that group.

The riddle of economic growth, then, is not the failure of LDCs to grow, but their success. Within that riddle lies the mystery of the great differences among LDCs in growth rates. They are not accounted for merely by differences in climate, education, the population-natural resource ratio, the rate of population growth or all of these, though no doubt these factors contribute their effects. This is the mystery to which Professor Mya Maung has addressed himself, selecting for his study the contrast between Burma, rich in natural resources, whose per capita income--after falling during World War II-- has not yet recovered to the level of 1939, and Pakistan, less well endowed--her economic system seriously disrupted in 1947 by the bifurcation of the economic system in which she had been enmeshed--whose growth rate has, nevertheless, been well above the world average. He has searched widely for the causes. He analyzes differences in the colonial impact, in social conflict, in development ideology, in religious ideology, in other aspects of culture and, at the greatest length, in differences in economic policy. Standing within his field of professional training, economics, he has also reached outside it.

I have known him since he came to the United States from Burma for graduate study, at about the time I returned--in 1953--from a period of professional work in Burma. This, his first book, whose topic is the subject-matter of his teaching, rests, in part, but only in part, on his knowledge of his native society and his ability to analyze that society dispassionately. His book will be of wide interest to scholars who are groping for explanations of differences in growth rates. Some students of economic development are not groping. They "know" that the dominant explanatory factor is the rate of investment, or training during a colonial period, or education or, even, climate. The difficulty with these certainties is that they ignore reality. Too many countries contradict any pat explanation. To scholars whose minds are open, which is to say to the great majority of scholars in the field, Mya Maung's analysis will provide stimulating suggestions.

Everett E. Hagen
Center for International Studies
Massachusetts Institute of Technology
Cambridge, Massachusetts

PREFACE

The primary purpose of this book is to answer the question of why certain types of economic philosophy and policy are being pursued in the countries of Pakistan and Burma and to examine their degree of success or failure. The book is also a beginning for future empirical research in comparative development. Needless to say, the processes and problems of development encompass an endless range of human activities, and the task of selecting pertinent variables and determinants is as complex as development itself. It is necessary, therefore, to mention some of the areas that the book cannot or does not cover.

Since the study is a macroanalysis of comparative development policies and results, specific intraregional and intragroup variations of culture within Burma and Pakistan are left largely untouched. Treating Pakistan as one unit without its East and West segments may be a flaw, yet the author finds it both impossible and irrelevant to delve into cultural plurality and ethnolinguistic differences. The cutoff point in this investigation is, therefore, set at a comparison of sociopolitical and economic structures, along with social conflict, as they affect the overall outlook, motivations and policies of development. With this view in mind, the study confines itself to the origins and causes of societal insulation and openness as they are reflected in the development policies of Burma and Pakistan.

The research grew out of a monograph prepared by the author for Professor John H. Badgley some three years ago. Since then, it has taken different forms and undergone various revisions. After presenting the main ideas at a number of seminars and receiving responses from former professors, associates and students, it has finally reached the stage of becoming a book. The successful appearance of this book owes a great deal to Professor Badgley, who helped me to get started, and to the momentum offered by the International Development Studies Program, Fletcher School of Law and Diplomacy, at Tufts University. I want to thank Professors Robert L. West, Robert F. Meagher, Robert F. Stephens and Allen B. Cole of that institution for providing me with a stimulating research environment, as well as their comments on various drafts of the study. Special thanks are also due to Miss Margaret P. Richardson for her meticulous and effective editing of the work.

The individuals who have given me inspiration and help are many. Among them, my former professors K. E. Boulding, H. W. Spiegel and the late Max F. Millikan deserve special gratitude for stimulating my interest in the social aspects of economic development. Of all the readers of the manuscript, Professor E. E. Hagen has given me the most careful comments, criticism and encouragement, without which the book would have never reached its final form. I would also like to extend my appreciation to my colleagues at Boston College for permitting me to consult at the Fletcher School and for giving me summer grants to do research. Last but not least, my wife, Marya, deserves all my thanks for giving hope and comfort in my struggle to complete this work for publication.

CONTENTS

ix

LIST OF TABLES

Burma and Pakistan: A Comparative Study of Development

CHAPTER **1** THE STATE OF THE
ECONOMICS OF
DEVELOPMENT

At the very outset, it will be noted that the state of the
economics of development is somewhat as underdeveloped as
the object of inquiry--the less developed countries (LDCs).
It is a common theme of contemporary inquiry into the poverty
of nations that theories and therapies based on the model of
advanced industrial countries and their development experiences in the past are inadequate or inapplicable to the problems
of development confronting the LDCs today. [1] Some attempts
have been made to mend conventional theories and reconstruct
the methodological framework of economic growth by means
of extensive analysis. Most of these attempts take the form
of either transforming parameters that are traditionally assumed to be beyond the realm of economics or incorporating
certain theories from other social sciences. The first approach reflects the view that the principles of economics
governing the process of development are neutral and valid in
spite of institutional variations among different societies.
The second approach stems from the holistic and institutional
view that the economic phenomenon of development or underdevelopment must be analyzed "not as a segment but as an aspect of the whole complex of social relationships. "[2]

Indeed, the field of economic development offers less attraction to those economists "who treat economics as a form
of applied mathematics. "[3] It is, of course, common knowledge
that economic development is a by-product of human endeavor,
encompassing an endless range of human activities and social
goals. The most crucial weakness of positive economics, as
it has developed in recent times, lies in its inability to cope
with the sociocultural matrix of development. Specialization
and division of labor, which have served as the basis for
economic development, have their counterparts in social
studies, where social processes are treated in a mechanistic
way in terms of quantifiable variables. Like that of the developed countries' social structure, economic system, outlook

3

and value systems, the economic discipline has been oriented
to the technical aspects of material culture. Precisely due
to this orientation and methodological development, the study
of LDCs, where paucity of statistical data is not the exception
but the rule, has been one of those frustrating, empty, economic
boxes to model-building economists. As a result, the economics of development suffers from a poverty of knowledge
and general theory, which could provide foundations for the
formulation of sound policies of development.

Current polemical discussions on the process, problem
and strategy of economic development reflect not only the
need for formal recognition but also for treating the so-called
noneconomic determinants of economic development in the
form of a system analysis. [4] This appears to be due to a large
residue of unexplained qualitative factors--technological progress, for instance, which is considered to be the most important determinant in the economic transformation of traditional pretechnological societies, and the belief that social
theories in disciplines other than economics have reached a
state of maturity for an integrated approach. [5] (Whether or
not social theories in such disciplines as sociology, social
anthropology, social psychology and others have reached a
state of maturity is still a debatable issue, since they all seem
to suffer from the same problem--lack of a general theory--
as the economics of development.) This trend of extensive
analysis, in contrast to intensive analysis by means of simplified theoretical models, derives its vigor and importance from
the anxiety and urgency with which the underdeveloped countries have striven, and often failed, to achieve economic progress and the feeling of inadequacy and frustration of those who
are called upon to diagnose the problems of underdevelopment
and prescribe policies for development.

The contemporary ethos of the economics of development
is overwhelmed with imports, and the integration, of various
theories from other social disciplines--particularly, social
anthropology and psychology--to meet the challenge of extensive analysis. Economists and other social scientists alike
incorporate each other's theories and methods without being
entirely wertfrei from disciplinary biases and predilections. [6]
This effort to reap the benefits of specialization and division
of labor in social studies is not really a new phenomenon. In
a way, it is only a reinforcement of the concrete foundation
and precedent laid down by Adam Smith, Karl Marx, Werner
Sombart, Max Weber, Vilfredo Pareto, Joseph Schumpeter,
R. H. Tawney, Thorstein Veblen and a host of other economists.

Recent criticisms of the classical and neoclassical theories
of economic growth, the theory of vicious circles, the take-off
theory and stages of economic growth and critiques of capital-
stock adjustment theory[7] all share the inadequacy of existing
economic theories in dealing with human or social elements
in the process of economic change.

Methodological innovation along the lines of extensive
analysis of social factors, however, has been equally tiresome
and frustrating. As A. O. Hirschman complains: "The intensive study of economic development has had one discouraging
result: it has produced an ever-lengthening list of factors and
conditions, of obstacles and prerequisites."[8] Although this
statement contains a grain of truth, it is also true that the very
discovery of such a list tends to break down the analytical confinement to pure economic factors as such. It is quite correct
that a sheer extension of the methodological framework for its
own sake may be worse than no extension at all. Indeed, "A
synthesis of inadequate parts may be worse than no synthesis
at all."[9] This, of course, is one inescapable dilemma of the
methodological choice between general and particularized ap-
proaches--the Marshallian trees and the forest--which runs
through all social studies. In the economics of development,
this problem is further complicated by the need to descend
from the level of theory and abstraction to reality, especially
in the realm of strategy and policy where assumptions fail to
hold true.

From "classical magnificent dynamics" to the post-
Keynesian macroeconomic models of growth, the dilemma of
the logical versus the real has been evaded by a distinction
between the "organon of pure analysis" and evolutionary or
applied economics. As Adam Smith and David Ricardo considered changes in wants, resources and technology as belong-
ing to the higher theme of historical or evolutionary economics,
so Marshall and Keynes also explicitly recognized the importance of applied economics. [10] In a sense, the triumph of the
"Keynesian revolution" was not so much in the realm of pure
analysis but of applied economics, thereby challenging the behavioral postulates of classical and neoclassical economics.
Although, in some respects, recent methodological ventures
into the realm of the social reality of economic development
may be rewarding, the newness of such ventures cannot be
fully accredited as revolutionary. In the words of R. H.
Tawney, "In the present century, the old issues seem, indeed,
to have acquired a new actuality."[11] Those economic boxes
are, therefore, not so empty in traditional pretechnological

societies, where the weltanschauung, science, technology and economy are found to be inextricably intertwined.

The above view is not shared by R. A. Dahl and C. E. Lindblom, who seem to conclude that "in economic organization and reform, the great issues are no longer the great issues, if ever they were."[12] If this means that economic and social problems are a function of the time and type of the society, the case for the value-neutrality of a functional approach to economic change is not very strong. If it means that functionalism has dominated methods of economic analysis, however, it is doubtless a positive assertion on the present state of economics and studies of economic development. The use of a structural-functional approach in economic development is largely due to two interrelated forces: dissatisfaction at the simplified macroeconomic models of growth and the desire to develop a comprehensive general theory of social change and economic development.

The eruption of a functional spirit in the economics of development is late in comparison to the methodological history of sociology. In sociology, the growth of functional analysis has been oriented toward cumulative theories of social change as a reaction to evolutionary global theories of the early twentieth century.[13] In dealing with the problems and processes of economic development, special attention must be given to the application of a structural-functional approach. A functional concept of society has led many socioeconomists to develop cumulative theories of economic change, exemplified in such hypotheses as circular causation, vicious circles, forward and backward linkages and stages of economic growth.

The major defects of such theories, as pointed out by sociologists, are exaggerations of structural and functional unity, continuity and teleology. In particular, they tend to exaggerate the eufunctional and static character of pretechnological societies. They also seem to imply that the sustained economic growth of technologically matured economies is static. (W. E. Moore's critique of the Rostowian takeoff and three-stage model of economic growth may be taken as a case in point.)[14] Most serious of all, these cumulative theories offer very little in the way of effective formulation of development policies, except for the popular aphorism that "nothing fails like failure" or "nothing succeeds like success." Without belittling the concept of a circular constellation of the causes of poverty or the principle of mutual causation between what is economic and what is noneconomic in the process of social change, it is certain that the economics of development needs more than purely functional theories of circular causation.

The alternative to a functional theory lies in the quest for the origins and sources of socioeconomic change. The inevitable pitfall of such an approach to the organic growth of social systems is its possible culmination in a model of cumulative retroactive evolution. In order to avoid this, R. K. Merton and P. A. Sorokin have suggested the synthesis of a structural-functional concept with an organic concept of a given social system viewed in its historical perspective. One must maintain that the process of socioeconomic change is an explicit function of some standardized social items, which may be one or many, depending upon the analytical interest and constraints of the model. These might include "social roles, institutional patterns, social processes, cultural patterns, culturally patterned emotions, social norms, group-organization, social structure, devices of social control, "[15] and so forth. For the analytical purpose of this study, the particular social phenomenon of "social conflict" is chosen to explain the reasons for the relative success or failure of development programming in Burma and Pakistan.

Historically, economic analysis has been oriented toward the mechanistic and atomistic concept of social systems. The major reason for this must be sought in the value-premise and desire of economists to divorce the natural from the moral, or the positive from the normative, in their study of the origin and nature of a nation's wealth. From the Smithian "invisible hand" and "atomistic competition" through neoclassical "free competition" and modern theories of "pure competition" and "full-employment equilibrium, " the postulate-deductive form of equilibrium theory and method tends to pervade the economic universe. The economic system, like the technocratic social system of advanced countries, has become a universe of goods and services rather than of men. The main focus of economic analysis tends to be on "those things, material and immaterial, which are produced, distributed, exchanged, and consumed, rather than in the producers, distributors, exchangers, and consumers as people. "[16] The defect of such a development-- as exemplified in the postulates of rational, economic man: maximization of utility and return, perfect knowledge and interpersonal comparison of utility--is common knowledge in modern economics. From this knowledge, a clue emerges as to why conventional economic theories fail in the analysis of the poverty of nations: the subjugation of behaving economic units (human beings) to mechanically conceived activities, such as saving, investment and consumption, has, traditionally, been the key defect of economic analysis.

The most crucial point in reconstructing a methodological framework of economics to meet the challenge of extensive analysis is to treat the economic system not only as one of economic activities but also as one of social relationships among various economic agents. In analyzing the question of social obstacles to economic change, this study seeks to define the missing element of relating economic activities and variables to behavioral social groups in a particular society. The emphasis on technology and purely technical aspects of economic change, which characterizes modern capitalism, as opposed to the emphasis on social and political aspects in Marxian socialism, [17] may be used as a point of departure in analyzing why certain LDCs adopt socialism or capitalism in the modernization process.

In spite of common insistence that development theories and policies based on the model of an advanced country are inapplicable to the problems confronting the LDCs, there is a fascinating aspect to the development attempts by the LDCs that, in fact, imitate and apply the three basic models of an economic system--modern capitalism, the welfare state and the Sino-Soviet command economy. Although there are institutional variations in the adoption of these models, analysis of economic development in the LDCs has often been made in terms of the relative efficiency of these three economic systems. Understanding why certain LDCs absorb and experiment with certain types of economic policy and systems is highly important in the analysis of the poverty of nations. With this objective in mind, I have chosen Burma and Pakistan as two contrasting economic systems, one based on modern capitalism and the other on Sino-Soviet socialism in the process of modernization. The major concepts and analytical framework of the study follow.

SOCIAL CONFLICT AND ECONOMIC CHANGE

(1) For analytical purposes, the process of economic change may be treated as an aspect of social change from a given state of socioeconomic conditions to another in the historical plane. The general pattern of socioeconomic change may be conceived of as a process of dynamic social conflict and conflict-resolution among various social groups, invariably involving changes in wants, resources, technology and value systems. The higher level of economic performance of a

particular social system at particular points of time in history is not simply a function of available material resources but also of widening the sociocultural horizon. In fact, the socio-cultural matrix of development is to be found in the process of social conflict that took place within and without a social system. The higher level of economic performance of a society is a function of two general determinants: demand and capacity. Changes in demand are revealed in a higher propensity to consume, invest, exchange and trade on the part of important social groups, whose sociopolitical and economic roles, status and motivations form the basis of modernization. These groups might be the state, the civil society, the aliens, the majority, the minority, the military or the civil service. Changes in capacity are reflected in a higher propensity to save, innovate, produce and organize by these groups. Generally, a transitional state of socioeconomic change is marked by social conflict, the resolution of which is a prerequisite for development. The process of social conflict between any two traditional societies varies according to their respective sociopolitical and cultural heritages and their patterns of social relationships.

(2) A social system may be viewed as a system of social relationships, while the economic, political and cultural systems only reflect some aspects of certain types of social relationships. Economic development is affected by changes in the given social relationships that take place within a society as a result of social contact, conflict and change initiated by particular social groups. This process may evolve through the exposure of society to outside forces or through the socioeconomic mobility of certain social groups within the social system. In the case of colonial subjugation, social conflict between the ruler and the ruled usually takes the form of "status withdrawal" on the part of the traditional social system as a whole. The impact of colonization also differs from society to society with respect to how social relationships are maintained and changed by the colonial power, on the one hand, and the nature of the basic social conflict and relationships, on the other.

(3) We may take any two points of time in history and determine their respective sets of social relationships to designate two different states of sociopolitical and cultural development, then analyze the process of social conflict and change. If these represent the process of economic takeoff, an analysis of the intermediate states of tension-management within and without a social system must be made to explain the sources of high social propensity to develop.

The sources of social change for economic development--
which could be the exposure of society to international trade,
international conflict, colonial expansion and subjugation, internal social conflict and warfare--may be classified as either
exogenous or endogenous. The outergenerated social change
is clearly discernible in the process of colonization and the
deliberate import of alien technology, capital and social groups,
while the innergenerated social change is revealed in the intergeneration conflict, intragroup conflict and politicocultural
revolutions. Though these two types of social change are
analytically distinguishable at particular points of time in the
historical individuation of a country, the dynamics of social
change for economic development is a process of continual
social conflict and conflict-resolution between the exogenous
and endogenous social forces. Economic development ultimately
entails a social change internal to the social system, as R. A.
Nisbet observed:

> When we say that a culture or institution or nation
> 'grows' or 'develops,' we have reference to change
> in time, but to change of a rather special and dis-
> tinctive type. We are not referring to random and
> adventitious changes, to changes induced by some
> external deity or other being. We are referring to
> change that is intrinsic to the entity, to change that
> is held to be as much a part of the entity's nature
> as any purely structural element. Such change may
> require activation and nourishment from external
> agencies, just as does the growth in a plant or
> organism. But what is fundamental and guiding
> is nonetheless drawn from within the institution
> or culture. [18]

Indeed, from this point of view it is clear why a simple
imitation of advanced socioeconomic systems or importation
of foreign capital and technology cannot and does not induce
economic transformation. The wealth and economic growth
can only be explained by a lack of effective social and cultural
growth (in the above-mentioned sense) among the LDCs.
     (4) At this juncture, it becomes necessary to determine
what kind of social conflict and change impede or enhance
development. It is quite common in recent studies on economic
development to point out that the sociopolitical and cultural
framework of traditional societies is not conducive to modernization. The question then is: What, precisely, is the proper

social framework for development? The answer to this question has been as difficult and frustrating as the problem of development itself. The absence of any model of so-called world culture[19] that is suitable for modernization makes it all the more difficult to determine the form and substance of a viable culture. Perhaps, it is not the sociopolitical and cultural systems but the ways in which particular social groups set certain standards of actions and patterns of social relationships that account for relative lags in development. To answer this complex problem of what constitutes a viable culture, we must determine how certain social groups come to dominate the social system and how they resolve the social conflict between tradition and modernity.

(5) In the light of the process of social conflict within a society, lags in entrepreneurship and differences in the so-called achievement motivation, acquisitiveness and status withdrawal seem to convey important meaning. For classification of social structures by such prototypes as achievistic, ascriptive[20] and acquisitive adds very little to the analysis of relative achievements in modernization among the LDCs. In particular, there seems to be no correlation between social structure and the types of economic and political systems adopted by the LDCs. Not all highly authoritarian social structures have inhibited innovation, acquisitiveness and achievement, nor have all egalitarian social structures been conducive (or susceptible) to the development of an acquisitive, capitalist society. One finds, therefore, a country with no caste system and a landed aristocracy embracing the Sino-Soviet brand of socialism, while a highly stratified and class-conscious society follows the path of modern capitalism, as in the cases of Burma and Pakistan.

(6) The adoption of certain types of economic policy and development goals by the LDCs is not necessarily a simple function of the Marxian mode of production and dialectical materialism but of complex social changes, conflicts and relationships, along with traditional cultural heritages and value systems of a traditional social system. The appeal of Marxian and modern socialism (or aversion to capitalism) in the LDCs lies in the process of social conflict, which is both economic and cultural. On the doctrinal level, the appeal of socialism to the nationalist political leadership is stronger than capitalism in that the value premises of the former seem to fit in with traditional views and value systems. In the case of colonial plural societies, the intrusion of aggressive, alien social groups plus the tension-management of colonial rule have

resulted in a pervasive carry-over effect of an aversion to
capitalism. Trade and entrepreneurial activities dominated
by alien social groups come to represent exploitation and the
loss of social status to the natives. In the postcolonial period,
this process of social conflict continues with differing intensity,
depending upon the nature and types of social change that
develop after the liquidation of colonial rule. In countries
where alien social groups continue to dominate the economic
system, the appeal of the Sino-Soviet approach to development
tends to be strongest.[21]

Closely linked to social conflict are traditional value systems, most of which contain elements of anticapitalism or
antimaterialism. The moral overtones of Marxism and modern
socialism seem to invoke traditional nationalism by fostering
a sense of national identity and moral integrity. Paradoxically,
it is not the materialism of Marxian socialism but such moral
sentiments as "to each according to his need," "exploitation
of the masses or the natives by greedy and immoral capitalists,
and "equality" that arouse the nationalist emotions of tradition-
bound elites and the masses alike. In a sense, calling for
drastic social and political revolution by socialism is more
evolutionary than revolutionary as far as the preservation or
resurrection of lost cultural heritages are concerned. In
other words, the cultural price that must be paid to modernize
seems less expensive in the moral light of socialism than of
capitalism.[22]

(7) Using an initial state of social solidarity in history,
social change and economic development may be viewed as a
dynamic process of disequilibria or disorganization, generated
by societal contact, cultural diffusion and repulsion. The success or failure of economic transformation may be explained
in terms of transmission of information and the entropy of
culture, or of the elasticity of the traditional social system
in its adaptability to the absorption of advanced alien technology
and value systems on the one hand and the nature and types of
social relationships that develop during the course of international social conflict on the other. The entropy of cultural
systems differs in terms of sociocultural constraints and the
variety of information gathered by the traditional social system.* A social system with minimal constraints in the

---

*This cybernetic law of communication, with respect to
the transmission of information and the transformation of the
operand, is commonly employed under different names in both
physical and social sciences. Physicists term it the law of

accumulation of a maximum variety of information may be
called open; the reverse is true of a closed social system.

The transmission of technological information from outside the social system takes many forms, among them the introduction of new goods, services, knowledge, techniques,
value systems and organizations. Elements such as these may
or may not come to be institutionalized in a traditional social
system, depending on the ways they are injected and the intensity of social conflict. In any event, the process of economic
change as an aspect of social change takes place with maximum
effect in the historical setting of an open society with an open
economy. In terms of international trade and economic relationships, an open economy is a necessity; however, it may
not be sufficient to generate the needed momentum in social
change required for effective technological transformation.
In many colonial plural societies of Asia and Africa, for instance, the economy is physically open, while the traditional
social system is closed with respect to the transmission and
absorption of an alien technology. The phenomenon of a dual
economy, resulting from the prolonged coexistence of modern
industry and traditional techniques, [23] reflects one aspect of
social conflict leading to a closed sociocultural system in
which social groups exist side by side with rigid barriers of
assimilation and cultural transfusion. To colonized and tradition-bound peoples, modern economic occupation, industry,
trade and practices represent not only a cultural threat through
possible destruction of the traditional family and value systems, [24] but also a cultural betrayal and actual political serfdom to the alien colonial power. The unfortunate result, of
course, is the underdevelopment of native entrepreneurship
and strong feelings of anticapitalism.

(8) For purposes of analyzing social conflict and economic
change, the terms "open" or "closed," in reference to a social
system, are not used here to mean a pure state of physical

------

motion; biologists, as ecological succession; economists, as
elasticity, absorptive capacity and demonstration effect;
sociologists, as social ecology and cultural diffusion; historians,
as the zeitgist, dialectics and various notions of progress.
See P. A. Sorokin, Social and Cultural Mobility (New York:
The Free Press of Glencoe, 1964), Appendix; Ragner Nurkse,
Problems of Capital Formation in Underdeveloped Countries
(Oxford: Basil Blackwell, 1957), pp. 61-67; and W. R. Ashby,
An Introduction to Cybernetics (New York: J. Wiley & Sons,
1963), pp. 174-86.

contact or isolation. As suggested, it is true that the problems
of development confronting the LDCs today are a by-product
of opening up the social system rather than closing it in complete isolation. [25] Yet what is central to the policy and strategy
of economic development is whether or not a traditional social
system, after a series of historical societal contacts with the
outside world, becomes open or closed culturally and ideologi-
cally in the process of becoming modernized. Those who close
or open a social system are certain social groups; their relationships, motivations and socioeconomic conflicts must be
analyzed in explaining the progress of modernization. For,
in fact, development plans and their relevant implementation
in the LDCs inevitably represent a disequilibrating wedge in
existing sets of social relationships among various social
groups or economic agents. The success or failure of economic
change can be analyzed and appraised in terms of the acceptance
of the principle of opportunity costs, which applies forcibly
to problems of modernizing and the preservation of traditional
institutions by the ruling political elite. To be sure, it is reluctance to pay the cultural price for modernization that deter-
mines the degree of openness of a given social system. From
a strategic point of view, any successful measure of socioeconomic change in a LDC requires effective transmission by
the ruling political elite of alien ideas, values and technology,
which will be socially and culturally acceptable to the masses.

(9) In contemporary theorizing on economic development,
an argument seems to be prevalent that stresses the need for
large-scale state intervention, control and planning in the light
of the shortage of resources--both human and nonhuman--a
theory built on the premise of an historic slumbering of LDCs
in the "Rip Van Winkle world" of relative economic stagnation,
while the Western world for many generations developed
rapidly. [26] It is also argued that this differential in initial
conditions between the LDCs today and the Western countries
in their early stages of economic transformation has made
"the challenge of state economic planning all the more
dramatic. "[27] Equally dramatic has been the frustration at
failures in planning, socializing and controlling the economy,
which are reminiscent of the historical experience of many
developed countries that have traveled similar paths of
modernization. Although the ideology of planning and control
serves as a rationalization for interventionist practices, the
actual fermentation of statecraft in planning is so slow and
defective that this rationalization remains, at best, an emotiona
matrix rather than an intellectual one. [28] It is neither sufficient

nor correct to state, as Gunnar Myrdal has done, that "many
of the inherited inequalities and rigidities are adverse to
economic development and need to be mitigated by coordinated
state policies if development is to be achieved. "[29]
     The precise problem of development by means of large-
scale state actions has been an inability to coordinate and
implement plans on the national level, in addition to the inequalities and rigidities of an LDC, including the state itself.
As Hla Myint correctly argues:

> There is no reason to suppose that economic
> policies considered appropriate for the advanced
> countries will prove to be equally appropriate to
> the underdeveloped countries. But this "realistic"
> objection to generalizations should apply not only
> to laissez-faire but also to the planning policies
> in the underdeveloped countries. [30]

     In rejecting the socioeconomists' criticism of the institu-
tional bases of orthodox economic theories, he further argues
that existing conventional theories of economic growth and
tools of analysis are quite relevant to the problems of development confronting the LDCs today: "The substitution of the
phrase 'planning agency' for the 'market mechanism' merely
glosses over the actual problems of mobilization and allocation
of resources according to the plan and, above all, the problems
of coordination and flexible adjustments. "[31]
     This position, however, is not quite as value-neutral as it
pretends to be, since a preference for the market mechanism
persists even among the most liberal-minded economists.
When the alternatives of Western versus Sino-Soviet approaches
to social change and economic development are confronted, the
greater weight given to the role of the market mechanism and
private sector creeps into the recommendations of most Western
economists. Such terms as "planning through market mechanism, " "the controlled economy" and "the welfare state" are,
at best, a compromise between the two basic economic systems
of pure capitalism and Sino-Soviet socialism. Indeed, the basic
dilemma of development policies and the actual adoption of
certain economic systems seems to be the relative roles of the
state and the private sector. Yet, economists are usually lost
when it comes to the problem of designing a model of social
change for rapid socioeconomic development.
     On the other hand, some social scientists are equally
uncertain about the best cultural model suitable for the

development of an achieving society. More often than not, one
finds the same kind of vicious circle of causation in theories
of social change. A high or low level of the so-called n
Achievement motive in a particular society may be associated
with a high or low level of technological civilization, which,
in turn, produces a high or low propensity to innovate. From
the theory of an achieving society to theories of innovational
versus authoritarian personality based on the microanalysis
of family-rearing habits, the authoritarian structure of traditional societies is often exaggerated to account for a lack of
an entrepreneurial function. [32] It is neither sufficient nor
valid to assert that "a high level of the n Achievement might
predispose any society to vigorous activity, " or "higher n
Achievement should be associated with higher technological
development. "[33] If modernization can be thought of as the
result of entrepreneurial activities of peoples with higher
achievement motivation in a particular society, then the nature
of the social system that permits these peoples to achieve
must be examined. In recent times, modernization has been
achieved through the suppression of peoples with such motivation. It is, therefore, paradoxical that a society with strong
authoritarian social and political structure, such as Russia
or China, was able to create a high level of n Achievement by
deliberate programs aimed at subduing private incentives to
innovation and entrepreneurial activities.

Anthropologists are not in total agreement with respect
to whether or not ascetic traditional religions tend to repress
innovation. The Weberian hypothesis of Protestant ethics and
the rise of capitalism is rejected equally by anthropologists
and economists, so that one cannot ascertain the sources of
high achievement motivation. [34] The solution to these incon-
sistencies in social theory lies in the study of social conflict
between traditional values and particular modern values, which
are needed for development, on the one hand, and among certain social groups, on the other. With this objective in mind,
this study contends that the degree of success in modernization
among the LDCs is a direct function of their ability to resolve
social conflict and the types of elites that come to dominate
the social system in its historical perspective.

(10) The natural outcome of most attempts to theorize
about the developmental process is a position of relative in-
stitutionalism. Most development economists argue that the
relevancy of either planning or the market mechanism to a
particular country is a function of the level of political and
cultural development. J. K. Galbraith states, with respect

to India, "India's present need for capital is not based on a low level of development. It is the result, as compared with other new nations, of a relatively high level of cultural and political development that enables her to use capital effectively."[35] Gustav Papanek makes this observation about Pakistan's development: "Neither development in Western Europe, when industrial technology was in its infancy, nor the experience of 'traditional,' stagnant societies may have much relevance for a country such as Pakistan, experiencing rapid change...."[36] A similar position is taken by Hla Myint who warns that "the first thing to bear in mind about the underdeveloped countries is that beyond the broad common fact of poverty it is rarely safe to make generalizations about them without carefully specifying the type of underdeveloped country one is considering."[37]

It goes without saying that generalizing is dangerous and, perhaps, "productive of waste, frustration and disappointment."[38] Yet, economists and other social scientists alike do generalize in applying theories and principles of socioeconomic change to their analysis and appraisal of development planning in the LDCs. Despite the relative position they took in guarding against the defects of generalization, the predilection for capitalism or socialism--or a blending of the two-- persists in various forms when it comes to the question of the roles of the state and private sector in the developmental process.

In particular, when the economic history of development is written, the question of the relative efficiency of a planned economy versus a market-oriented economy reappears in the form of tightening economic controls as opposed to dismantling these controls, or "inward-looking" versus "outward-looking" nations.[39] Indeed, economic history is usually presented in terms of cause and effect, as reflected in certain economic actions and policies pursued by the state. Thus, the performance of the economy under the management of different ruling governments has been the main theme of historic appraisal of various economic miracles or disasters.

Despite the fallacy of post hoc ergo propter hoc, which politicians are apt to commit in their use of economic history, it is still important to determine the general course of economic events shaped by common factors of socioeconomic policies and actions among the LDCs.[40] It is also important to note that development planning in many LDCs is an aspect of the international mobility ideology and culture and that development planning in these countries is, more often than not, an

importation of advanced models from outside economic systems.
The economic history of advanced countries in their early
stages of development is, therefore, quite significant and
relevant in analyzing and assessing the problems of development confronting those LDCs that choose certain types of
economic systems as models for development. The crucial
questions to be answered are the following: (a) Why does a
particular LDC import one model of development instead of
another--a command economy, for instance? (b) What is the
sociocultural matrix for adopting certain economic policies
and effectively implementing these policies? (c) How do
social systems and social groups respond to specific socioeconomic actions undertaken by specific social groups? The
answer to these questions lies in the study of dynamic social
conflicts within and without a social system historically.

A GENERAL ANALYSIS OF
SOCIOECONOMIC CHANGE

     The history of economic transformation in many tradi-
tional societies is not a simple process of abrupt and autono-
mous growth of inventions, innnovations and new technology,
but a dynamic process of complex sociopolitical and cultural
changes at various points of time in history. For economic
development is more than a simple process of capital accumulation, increased productivity and optimum allocation of resources; it is also a process of changes in wants, values,
motivations and social relationships. Only within the framework of an open society or an open economy does the story of
spectacular takeoffs or relative lags in the economic growth
of many societies lend itself to rational analysis. (Incidentally,
the pattern of socioeconomic transformation does not reveal
definite stages with respect to either specific types of production and economy or standardized sociocultural systems.
Many pretechnological societies pass through a series of transitional states of chaos and disequilibria at different points in
historical time. The nature and duration of these transitional states vary from society to society, depending upon the
solidity of traditional culture, the type of societal contact with
economically advanced societies and the given state and nature
of a particular social system.)
     The social propensity to innovate is determined by the
elements of subsocial systems, such as the status, role and

functions of the household, community, state, elite, civil
society or deviant cultural brokers. From the ancient civilizations of the Egyptians, Babylonians, Aegeans and Sino-Indians
through the Phoenician, Greco-Roman, European, Western
and Sino-Soviet social systems, socioeconomic transformation
in many traditional societies is an integral part of the overall
process of transfusion, imposition, absorption, repulsion
and individuation of new values, technologies and ways of life.
It is in this sense that no existing society can be considered
as spontaneous and neutral with respect to its historic origins
and cultural configurations.

Causes of Advance or Lag of Economic Growth

Maturity of Sociopolitical and Cultural Changes

Recent studies on the comparative economic transformation of many countries seem to point out that maturity or com-
pletion of sociopolitical and cultural changes in a particular
society is the cause of either the advance or lag of economic
growth. [41] For example, many historians and economists
view the era of mercantilism as a prolonged transitional state
of social change and, subsequently, regard the date of the
Industrial Revolution as indeterminate. [42] Great Britain's
priority in economic takeoff has been attributed to a sociopolitical and cultural framework that was conducive to the up-
surge of technological inventions and economic innovations in
the late eighteenth century. Explanations for the development
of capitalism in England range from social theories of the rise
of liberalism, Protestant ethics, philosophy of the Enlightenment and class struggles to economic theories of inventions,
the discovery of iron and steel, external trade, international
division of labor and laissez-faire. The relatively early development of a high propensity to innovate in England cannot
be explained by purely economic reasons of specialization,
division of labor and extent of the market; nor can it be explained by a question-begging epitaph of fulfillment of preconditions. While the former suffers from the defect of functional teleology, the latter reflects the fallacy of petitio
principii.
The pronounced capability of the British social system to
innovate was a function of both physical and cultural setting
with respect to its historic openness. Not until the end of
mercantilism did the traditional social system of Britain lose

its sociopolitical and cultural constraints, by virtue of greater
contact, conflict and communication with the outside world.
The British cultural heritage was also heterogeneous and
elastic, in the sense of continuous societal contact, conflict
and absorption.

It is only in this light that centuries of prolonged transitional states in England can be traced back to forces that were
at work at the close of the Middle Ages. [43] The British system
was by no means bestowed with innate qualities of innovation
in the Smithian sense of man's natural proclivity and propensity "to trade, barter, and exchange one thing for another."[44]
It was, however, elastic and receptive to the creation and absorption of new technology. From the very beginning of its
Anglo-Saxon cultural configuration--from the Roman invasion
and the Danish and Norman conquests to the Crusades, One-
Hundred-Years War, the Seven-Year War and other inter-
European warfare--Great Britain's accumulation of technology
and the continuous widening of social and economic horizons
laid the foundation for the high propensity to "truck, barter,
and exchange." In this overall process, the absorption of
Calvinistic ethics, the Puritan Revolution, mercantilism and
economic liberalism can only be explained by the legacy of
conflict, acculturation and variety of information accumulated
and renovated in the historical setting of an open social system.

It has been observed that a fairly advanced agricultural
system was known to the Anglo-Saxons. As far back as the
ninth century, the land systems of sulung, furlung, and hyde--
far more advanced than some of the neolithic systems of underdeveloped countries today--were found to be prevalent in the
Kingdom of Kent. The mill (mylen, from Latin molina),
coinage, towns and roads in Britain also bear the imprint of
the Roman invasion. [45] This is not to imply that technological
transformation is simply a process of accumulation without
innovation. As the sum total of knowledge, science or art,
technology, rather, has the unique quality of evading the second
law of thermodynamics, by means of evolution, renovation and
innovation in an open social system. [46]

Degree of Openness of Social System

But even this is not the whole story of socioeconomic
change in England. Once a traditional social system is concretized into a state of equilibrium, with elapsing of time and
the establishment of institutions, repulsive and rigid constraints are also created. In Great Britain, the conflict

between the old and the new persisted to resist social change,
resulting in such transitional disequilibria as feudalism, the
Peasant Revolt of 1318, the rule of force by monarchy, the
contest between the Crown and Church, the civil wars of the
early seventeenth century, the Puritan Revolution, the social
and political emancipation of 1688 and the growth of laissez-
faire. In this light, the British economic takeoff is one of
the longest in the history of development. As for its priority
relative to other Western societies, it would seem that it was
due more to the higher degree of openness of the British
social system than to the innate quality of man as such.[47]

The economic transformation of the United States is an
exemplary case of social transfusion and historic openness
in the social system, which accounted for both a shorter
transitional state and weaker resistance to sociopolitical
changes prior to the economic takeoff. If one considers the
pre-Civil War period (before 1863) as that in which all the
preconditions to economic takeoff were laid down and sets
the achievement of technological maturity by about 1900, the
economic transformation of the United States becomes one of
the fastest in the economic history of the world.[48] The only
plausible reason for such a spectacular rate of economic
change, relative to England for example, is found in the in-
herently high propensity to innovate of the American social
system from the very beginning of its historic origin and to
the incessant flow of information and lack of repulsion during
the course of its development. Linkage to the Puritan Revolution in England and elsewhere,[49] the multicultural intermingling, the variety of sources of technological and cultural
information, the inheritance of already developed technology
and the ethnocultural heterogeneity throughout United States
history are all determinants of elasticity in a social system
that escaped from sociocultural constraints in its economic
transformation. This is, essentially, in line with the concept
of the "tradition-born-free society" of America, whose open
social system formed the key to its economic takeoff. As
the land of opportunity, America has enjoyed freedom and
flexibility from the very beginning of its historic inception,
in terms of both sociopolitical constraints and religious-
cultural inhibition against the pursuit of economic opportunities
and wealth. The philosophy of pragmatism that is associated
with the names of Peirce, James and Dewey and the philosophy
of Enlightenment that is embodied in the Declaration of Independence and the Constitution testify to the fact of cultural
elasticity in the American experience.

It is only in the above sense that the concept of a "tradition-born-free America" lends itself to rational analysis of
socioeconomic change. The agrarian myth of the yeoman
farmer as the ideal citizen might not have been strong enough
to act as the kind of constraint against such commercial realities as making money, saving, and agricultural innovation that
would have engendered a closed social system in early
America. [50] This myth, however, is still a reality in many
closed subsocial systems and regions of America today. The
Jeffersonian agrarian bias--a variant of the Smithian noble
country gentleman--found its fullest expression in "the instinct
of workmanship" and "conspicuous consumption" of Thorstein
Veblen.[51] Modern forms of this traditional prediliction are
mirrored in the family farm image and rational cultural biases
against ruthless money making, big business, industry and the
rat race of the congested and slummy metropolis. Indeed,
traditional sociopolitical and cultural constraints on economic
change in regionally underdeveloped areas of America today--
the Appalachian, deep South and Great Plains states, for
example--assume a spectacular parallelism with those of
many underdeveloped countries.

   Even this is not the entire story of cultural repulsion in
America. The case of the American Indians offers an example
of closed social systems within the "tradition-born-free
society. " It was to counteract alien cultural intrusion that the
tradition-bound American Indians plunged into a secluded closed
social system of apathy and indignation. Repulsion to the
cultural invasion of the "pale face" was further enhanced by
the ways in which social barriers were erected by both the
dominant and the dominated. Parallel examples of social
pluralism and cultural apathy can be found in many colonized
societies of Asia and Africa.

   Resistance of traditional sociopolitical and cultural systems to the penetration of new values and technology may be
viewed as a primary cause of relative lag in the economic
transformation of many European countries. The relatively
late economic transformation of France, Germany and Russia,
as opposed to Great Britain, for example, is often explained
by the lateness of social change. [52] However, this explanation
is not meaningful, unless the reasons for a late or low propensity to innovate are spelled out. Comparative examination
of historical circumstances and social conditions in these
countries reveals that different factors circumscribed the
relative lag in economic transformation. Religious intolerance
and miscalculation in warfare in France; political instability

in Germany, due to a mosaic of petty states and lack of national unification; and the rule of force and continuous international warfare of the Czars, who kept the Russian peasantry under the economic slavery of the pomeshchiki--all are historical situations that reflect different reasons for the lateness of economic change. Underlying these obstacles, however, is the principal parameter of a closed traditional society that is maintained and preserved by dominant social groups and the masses alike. Indeed, the intensity of the violence with which such societies transform socially is usually stronger once the "alienated elite"[53] has accomplished the sociopolitical awakening of the masses.

Both the Russian Revolution and the revolution of Communist China exemplify a prolonged closing of the social system to the penetration of outside values and technology and the later opening of the social system to the absorption of Marxian doctrines and modern technology. Inasmuch as the economic transformation of the Soviet Union is a history of deliberate planning, it is also a history of social change in the absorption and imposition of new values and technology. But to evaluate the spectacular achievement of the Soviet economic system only by concentrating on the efficiency of economic planning misses the point, for it minimizes the importance of sociopolitical and cultural changes that took place long before the New Economic Policy era. *

Comparison of Economic Development of China and India

Comparative studies of the economic development of China and India appear to suggest that China's greater achievement in recent years is due to the greater efficiency of a planned economy along the lines of the Soviet model. Yet stories of the spectacular technological advance of Communist China based on this reasoning fail to consider the long and

---

*There are two opinions as to the real takeoff of the Russian economy. Many economists consider the Russian economy of the 1920s as underdeveloped as the underdeveloped economies of today; some, however, date the Russian takeoff as far back as 1860, or about the time of the Stolypin Reform. W. W. Rostow, Schwartz, Buchanan and Ellis hold the latter view. This view, from the standpoint of social dynamics and economic development, is more appropriate for analysis.

difficult processes of sociocultural change that took place both
before and after the Communist Revolution.[54] The success
of China's economic development planning, relative to India,
is better explained by the priority of social reforms and forced
cultural changes in pre- and post-Communist China. It has
been observed that the impact of Western ideas and technology
had already shattered the traditional social system to a significant degree in pre-Communist China, thus providing a
favorable framework for social change and economic development;[55] in India, on the other hand, resistance to social change,
built up during the colonial period, has continued in the form
of anti-Western sentiment and the nationalist neutralism shown
by Indian leaders. The Bamboo Curtain, therefore, may be
a political reality but a social myth in terms of the absorption
of Western ideas and technology by Communist China. As
C. K. Yang remarks,

> In China, where a new economic pattern was being
> introduced from the West, it was the ideological
> promotion of a modern economy that formed the
> first step; and changes in some of the economic
> aspects of the family system stemmed from
> ideological agitation rather than from the immedi-
> ate pressure of a new economic environment
> [created by the Communist leadership].[56]

It might seem difficult to argue that the impact of the
West on China was more shattering in terms of the traditional
sociocultural system than it was in India. In retrospect, one
can see that differences in the degree of openness of the two
social systems is due both to the nature of historical societal
contact and to China's lesser degree of sociocultural constraint within the traditional social system. In the first place,
unlike India, the historical societal contact of China with the
technologically superior Western powers involved no single
force of colonialism that might engender a rigorously closed
social system. As far back as the sixteenth century, a
plurality of alien intrusion--particularly Russian and British--
took place in the process of technological diffusion through
trade relationships. From the establishment of the Sino-
Russian Treaty of Nerchinsk in 1689 through the eighteenth-
century Kiakhta Trade period to Chinese industrialization in
the nineteenth century, Russia, England and Japan played a
prominent role in diffusing complex technological information
into China.[57]

Second, with the passing of the traditional political system of China after the decline of the Manchu Dynasty and the coming of the Empress Dowager to power, the Chinese social system experienced a Westernization process that was by no means without violent social conflict. The absence of an alien colonial power and social groups, however, failed to produce massive cultural antipathy. [58]

Third, the pluralistic religious and secularized philosophical systems of China--such as Confucianism, Taoism and a system of ancestor worship--have not allowed the ascetic Buddhist religion to mold the Chinese masses into a society that is culturally indignant about acquisitiveness and trade. In the case of India, apart from the deeply rooted force of Hinduism, which has served as a repelling factor to Westernization, both culturally and politically, the rigorous caste system has produced barriers against internal social and cultural mobility by limiting the process of economic change via outer-generated social change. The social conflict of India with British colonial power was, therefore, more intensive and longer in duration than the Chinese counterpart.

This is not to argue that Hinduism or similar ascetic religions completely inhibit absorption of alien economic practices with respect to the pursuit and acquisition of wealth. Despite the distinction between religion in theory and practice or between the ethics of clergy and laity, there is ample historical evidence that many a church in various cultures has enjoyed a high economic standard and wealthy position relative to traditional civil society. Concurring with W. A. Lewis that nowhere in the world are laymen reluctant to seize better opportunities for material living, [59] one must be cautious about minimizing the role of religion in shaping the economic effort of a people in a specific historical situation. Without engaging in the controversial discussion of whether or not Hinduism possesses worldly traditions, it may be safely stated that the type of colonial impact on India has tended to intensify traditional sociopolitical and cultural constraints, thereby creating a more closed social system.

Economic Transformation of Japan

The process of social change and economic development in other traditional societies of Asia may be analyzed in the same framework of social dynamics. The economic transformation of Japan offers the best example of social innovation

achieved through conflict-resolution between what is completely
new, different and alien and what is old. (Indeed, it represents
a spectacular social transformation if one takes into view those
famous words of Rudyard Kipling: "East is East and West is
West, and never the twain shall meet." Apart from Japan,
Kipling's thought rings true in many traditional societies of
Asia, where resistance to the intrusion of Western values has
often resulted in a prolonged state of tension, violence and
apathy, loaded with contradiction and uncertainty.)

It may seem puzzling that the impact of traditional culture
upon the social propensity of Japan to innovate is rather weak
in contrast to either India or Burma. Clearly, however,
Japan has been exposed to the outside world as a free society,
and the role of traditional values is historically subdued by
the ruling elite. In the first place, the religious foundation
of Japan was pluralistic. Both Buddhism and Confucianism
penetrated into traditional Japanese society;* but they formed
only one aspect of the Japanese culture, which was built primarily on a solid foundation of Shintoism and a system of
secularized values, controlled and regulated by the ruling
political body, the imperial court. [60]

Historically, the impact of Shintoism--of loyalty to lords
and emperors--on the Japanese value system far outweighed
the ethics of either Buddhism or Confucianism in the evolution
of the Japanese social system. Long before the Meiji Restoration, the Japanese cultural system was more oriented to
secular values than to such Buddhist ethics of compassion as
suffering, contentment and impermanency. The Bushido
("The Way of the Warrior") of the samurai-bureaucrats is an
exemplary case of cultural innovation that may be compared
to some aspects of the Protestant ethic in deviating from
strict religious discipline. In the seventeenth and eighteenth
centuries, rediscovery of Confucianism--in the form of neo-
Confucianism--was further synthesized into a rational philosophy in which the Bushido and the Shido ("The Way of the
Samurai") were codified into ethical norms of conduct. (The
intellectual trend toward neo-Confucianism, associated with
such names as Yamaga Soko, was a culmination of the movement against Buddhism, which was considered antithetical to

---

*The Buddhism of Japan is Mahayana Buddhism (Chinese
in origin), in contrast to the Theravada Buddhism of Ceylon,
Burma and Thailand. Besides the popularly known Zen
Buddhism, there are many branches and sects of Mahayana
Buddhism in Japan, which create a heterogeneous religious
structure.

Confucianism in the peaceful era of the Tokugawa.)[61] Despite
the naturalization of the ethics of Confucianism, the native
cult of Shintoism continued to shape the Japanese social system. In the later phase of Tokugawa rule, the revival of pure
Shintoism led Japanese thinkers to search for a national cultural framework and a new identity for Japanese society.
Greater contact with Europe in the Tokugawa period and the
massive importation of Western culture and technology during
the Meiji Restoration led to many social reforms, which provided a social framework conducive to economic change.

The history of economic development in Japan is the
clearest example of sociocultural diffusion from outside, together with an open social system in terms of minimal constraints and a maximum variety of information absorbed and
renovated by a free and responsible political elite. By the
nineteenth century, Zen Buddhism ceased to be the official
religion of Japan, and secularization of religious ethics was
complete. Sociocultural change in Japan was initiated and accomplished on the societal level by the politically and socially
dominant elite; their alienation from the traditional cultural
system sometimes took the form of making religion and the
traditional cultural value system subservient to political purposes. The traditions of thrift and hard work in Japanese
culture supplemented the role of the state--or shogunate--in
modernizing Japan and produced an entrepreneurial function
among all classes of the social system. Not only the socially
displaced samurai, daimyo, Mitsui and Sumitomo aristocracy
but also individuals from the lower classes emerged as entrepreneurs, thereby laying the foundation for an acquisitive
society in Japan. [62]

To be sure, social change in pretechnological Japan was
by no means smooth and peaceful, nor was it accomplished by
the elite in a closed social system with no contact and conflict
with other social systems. Japan's societal contact with advanced countries of the West further enhanced cultural flexibility and a social propensity to innovate; contact with the
Western colonial powers was a free exchange of both conflict
and acculturation. The international setting of Japanese society
in the nineteenth century gave greater elasticity to socioeconomic change than that of many other Asian societies in the
same historical epoch. Such international factors as the development of the North Pacific trade route and the industrial
growth of the United States, the decay of the Manchu Dynasty
and the competition between Western colonial powers actually
strengthened Japan and contributed to a favorable climate for
social change, as well as an escape from colonial rule. [63]

Some Colonized Societies: Examples of Closed
Social Systems

Certain colonized societies of Asia offer examples of
closed social systems with strong resistance to the intrusion
of alien social groups, value systems and economic practices.
Their contact with Western colonial powers had certainly produced many changes. Yet, as far as the social diffusion of
new values and technology is concerned, there can be little
doubt that changes in the traditional sector of colonial plural
societies were ineffectual. In countries like India, Burma,
and Indonesia, protest against colonial rule gained its strength
from the deeply rooted religions of Hinduism, Buddhism and
Islam. For the immense impact of religion has been so great
that to the people of these societies, it is a way of life and a
culture in itself. This is not to imply that these religions are
innately incompatible with modern values or industrialization.
There have, for example, been dissenting views as to the impact of Hinduism on the Indian worldly tradition. [64]

Yet, it seems apparent that, in India, Burma and Indonesia,
religion forms a cultural substratum, which has not undergone
effective innovation or reformation in the manner of the Protestant Revolt. This is a de facto aspect of the kind of traditional society in which religion often serves as a unifying force
to repel the penetration of new values and economic practices.
Traditional cultural resistance to colonial intrusions took the
form of seeming indifference, and indignation, to economic
change, thereby leading to a prolonged period of "retreatism, "
or withdrawal from the currents of modern economic activities. [65] The result was what J. S. Furnivall defined as the
creation of "a plural society, " in which the dual economy exists
as an economic correlate. [66]

The essence of a colonial plural society lies in the structure and function of certain social groups, whose social relationships reflect more a social compound than a social mix-
ture. In terms of economic development, the indigenous
population functioned, more or less, in a closed social system,
while certain alien groups came to control strategic economic
activities. In the colonial plural societies of Southeast Asia,
the status and role of social groups were so distinctly differ-
entiated between alien groups--the Europeans, Indians and
Chinese--and the indigenous population that the tropical economy
functioned with traditional modes of operation. A small,
modern sector was created on top of the traditional sector,
producing a dual economy in which the need to innovate on the

part of the indigenous population was both socially and economically insignificant.

The lag in adjustment by the natives to a modern market
economy is, therefore, a function of two interrelated factors:
(a) traditional resistance to colonial intrusion resulting in
social and cultural antipathy toward profit-making business
enterprises and (b) the nature of colonial policy and practice.
In Burma, for example, the clerical order took the position
of rejecting anything alien--and, especially, Western values
and ways of life. Such words as myat-naphyu ("white face")
and sahphyu ("white letter") were common in colonial Burma.
(The word sahphyu connotes Christians; for example, the
Christianized ethnic group of Karens is called Sahphyu Kayin.)
These words suggest a strong cultural repulsion to the process
of Westernization.

A classic example of clerical antipathy to the emulation
of Western culture was its outright denunciation, and actual
destruction, of blouses made of an imported, thin, modern
fiber (padohnmah aingyi, "thin cotton blouse"). It was, indeed, quite a sight to see a monk chasing a young Burmese
maiden in the streets of Rangoon in the late 1930s to destroy
her blouse. (The Indians and Chinese were also labeled as
aggressive money-mongers, just as Jewish entrepreneurs
were resented by Gentiles in many Western societies.)

The history of political emancipation in Burma is directly
linked to its Buddhist cultural framework in the same manner
as Indian nationalist movements are linked to Hinduism. In
colonial Burma, the politicoreligious organizations of the
Young Men's Buddhist Association (established in 1906) and
the General Council of Buddhist Associations (established in
1912), the nationalist anti-British movements of the Thakins
("The Masters") and Doe-Bamah ("We Burmese") and the
political strike of the Buddhist monk, U Wisara, are a few
examples of political protests sanctioned and propelled by the
traditional cultural system of Buddhism. [67] In this social
climate of traditional protest and indignation, native social
groups subsisted as a separate social entity, thereby rendering,
in most Southeast Asian societies, a favorable economic environment for the economically more aggressive and socially
less resistant foreign Orientals.

The liberal economic policy of laissez-faire, exercised
by the colonial powers, did not help to prevent alien domination
of the modern sector of these dual economies. Colonial social
and economic policy both tended to uphold traditional institutions, while prolonging the coexistence of modern industry with

traditional techniques of production. For it was neither the
aim nor the desire of any colonial power to modernize the
plural society. The primary purpose of colonialism in Asia
was economic: to develop the extractive industries and primary
products of the dependencies in order to provide raw materials
needed by the metropoles. The technological transformation
of productive functions in these industries, therefore, was
unimportant. In addition, the abundance of cheap labor from
India and China contributed to the development of labor-
intensive methods of production, even in the small modern
sector of these economies. The term "coolies," alone, is
sufficient to show the labor-intensive production function in a
colonial dual economy.

Economic Activities of Foreign Orientals in Southeast Asia

The development of acquisitiveness and entrepreneurship
by Indian and Chinese peoples in Southeast Asian societies cannot be explained solely in terms of colonial policy and practice.
For Thailand is an example of a noncolonized traditional society
in which native entrepreneurship lags far behind the Chinese.
In the absence of social innovation, the condition of national
independence--which the current nationalist political leadership in the ex-colonies of Southeast Asia holds as the most
important prerequisite to economic transformation--is a
necessary, but not sufficient, precondition to economic takeoff. Thus, the reasons for the economic dominance of foreign
Orientals in Southeast Asia must be sought in the economic
and cultural factors that drove them to emigrate, plus freedom
from the cultural constraints of the society in which they
developed the entrepreneurial function. * I suspect that the
requirement of social innovation on the part of the Indians and
Chinese in their own environment is not less demanding than
on the part of the native populations of other Southeast Asian
countries.
        Indeed, one major reason for the enterprising economic
activities of colonial plural societies is their lack of the need

---

*The term entrepreneurship is used here in the sense of
a purposeful economic activity of an individual or social group
in initiating, participating in, maintaining and aggrandizing a
profit-oriented business. Cf. A. H. Cole, Business Enterprise
in Its Social Setting (Cambridge, Mass.: Harvard University
Press, 1959), p. 7.

to conform to social standards and their lack of sociopolitical
responsibility in resisting new value systems and economic
practices that had been introduced by the colonial powers.
Thus, they are usually found to be the most deviant and Westernized social groups in Southeast Asia. Between the natives
and the foreign Orientals, there was a time gap of both cultural
emulation and absorption of new values and technology. The
confrontation of the natives with the Western colonial powers
brought conflict and rejection. (Rejection is not necessarily
confined to Westerners per se; it encompasses all alien social
groups and resistance to almost any form of pressure for institutional change.) The confrontation between foreign Orientals
and the Europeans, however, was one of voluntary acquisition
of skill, knowledge and new values in the process of colonization. In addition, the lack of a strong cultural antipathy in an
alien land of economic opportunities laid the foundation for
their successful entrepreneurship. That is to say, the entrepreneurship of foreign Orientals in Southeast Asia "proceeds
in relationship to the situation internal to the unit itself, the
social group that really constitutes the unit, and to the economic,
political, and social circumstances--institutions, practices,
and ideas which surround the unit."[68] In short, the dominance
by aliens of the modern sector of dual economies in Southeast
Asia constitutes a social phenomenon the evolution of which
is caused and conditioned by the historical circumstances of
an open institutional order, the general state of social affairs
and the economic institutions of a traditional pretechnological
society.

NOTES

1. See Gunnar Myrdal, Economic Theory and Underdeveloped Regions (Bombay: Vors & Co., 1958), chap. ii;
also, his Asian Drama: An Inquiry into the Poverty of Nations
(New York: The Twentieth Century Fund, 1968), I, chap. i;
also A. O. Hirschman, The Strategy of Economic Development
(New Haven, Conn.: Yale University Press, 1959), chap. ii.

2. K. E. Boulding, A Reconstruction of Economics (New
York: J. Wiley & Sons, 1950), p. 4.

3. Stephen Enke, "Economists and Development: Redis-
covering the Old Truths," Journal of Economic Literature,
VII, 4 (December, 1969), 1125.

4. See E. E. Hagen, On The Theory of Social Change
(Homewood, Ill.: The Dorsey Press, 1963), pp. 4-8.

5. Ibid., pp. 49-51.

6. See Talcott Parsons and Neil J. Smelser, Economy
and Society: A Study in the Integration of Economic and Social
Theory (New York: The Free Press, 1965), pp. 30-32.

7. See Hagen, op. cit., pp. 42-43; also, Myrdal, Asian
Drama, III, Appendix 3.

8. Hirschman, op. cit., p. 1.

9. Boulding, op. cit., p. 50.

10. See J. M. Letiche, "Adam Smith and David Ricardo
on Economic Growth," B. F. Hoselitz, et al., Theories of
Economic Growth (New York: The Free Press of Glencoe,
1960), p. 66; also T. N. Hutchison, A Review of Economic
Doctrines (Oxford: Clarendon Press, 1953), pp. 71-77.

11. R. A. Tawney, Religion and the Rise of Capitalism
(New York: The American Library, 1961), p. 11.

12. R. A. Dahl and C. E. Lindblom, Politics, Economics
and Welfare (New York: Harper & Row, 1963), p. 3.

13. See W. E. Moore, "Theories of Social Change,"
American Sociological Review XXV, 6 (December, 1960),
810-12; also, P. A. Sorokin, Contemporary Sociological
Theories: Through the First Quarter of the Twentieth Century
(New York: Harper & Row, 1956), p. 195.

14. See W. E. Moore, Social Change (Englewood Cliffs,
N.J.: Prentice Hall, 1963), pp. 231-33.

15. R. K. Merton, Social Theory and Social Structure
(Glencoe, Ill.: Free Press, 1959), p. 50.

16. K. E. Boulding, "Welfare Economics," A Survey of
Contemporary Economics, ed., B. F. Haley (Homewood, Ill.:
R. D. Irwin, 1952), p. 3.

17. See Laura Randall, ed. , Economic Development: Evolution or Revolution? (Boston: D. C. Heath & Co. , 1965), p. viii.

18. R. A. Nisbet, Social Change and History: Aspects of the Western Theory of Development (New York: Oxford University, 1969), p. 7.

19. Cf. Lucien W. Pye, Politics, Personality, and Nation-Building: Burma's Search for Identity (New Haven, Conn.: Yale University Press, 1962), chap. i.

20. See Talcott Parsons, The Social System (Glencoe, Ill.: The Free Press, 1951), p. 182.

21. See C. K. Wilber, The Soviet Model and Underdeveloped Countries (Chapel Hill: North Carolina University Press, 1969), pp. 13-14.

22. Cf. J. K. Galbraith, Economic Development (Cambridge, Mass.: Harvard University Press, 1963), chap. iii.

23. Hirschman, op. cit. , p. 125.

24. See C. P. Kindleberger, Foreign Trade and National Economy (New Haven, Conn.: Yale University Press, 1964), chap. 14.

25. See Hla Myint, The Economics of the Developing Countries (New York: Frederick A. Praeger, Inc. , 1964), p. 23.

26. Myrdal, op. cit. , II, 710-20. From the theory of "balanced growth" to the thesis of "the big push, " it is assumed that the proper course of development actions is by large-scale state actions, in view of the relative lack of entrepreneurial talent and training in the private sector.

27. Ibid. , p. 715.

28. Cf. ibid. , p. 711.

29. Ibid. , p. 718.

30. Hla Myint, "Economic Theory and Underdeveloped Countries, " The Journal of Political Economy, LXXIII, 4 (October, 1965), 478.

31. Ibid. , p. 480.

32. David C. McClelland, The Achieving Society (Princeton, N. J. : D. Van Nostrand Co. , 1961), chap. i; also, Hagen,
op. cit. , chap. 18.

33. McClelland, op. cit. , pp. 63 and 65.

34. See Manning Nash, The Golden Road to Modernity:
Village Life in Contemporary Burma (New York: John Wiley
& Sons, 1965), chap. 9.

35. Galbraith, op. cit. , p. 48.

36. Gustav Papanek, Pakistan's Development: Social
Goals and Private Incentives (Cambridge, Mass. : Harvard
University Press, 1967), p. 47.

37. Hla Myint, op. cit. , p. 14.

38. Galbraith, op. cit. , p. 47.

39. Hla Myint, "Economic Theory and Development Policy,"
Economica, Vol. XXXIV (May, 1967); also, Papanek, op. cit. ,
chap. i.

40. See Introduction by J. Enoch Powell in J. Hennessy,
V. Lutz and G. Scimone, Economic "Miracles" (London:
Andre Deutsch, 1964), pp. ix-x.

41. See W. W. Rostow, The Stages of Economic Growth:
A Non-Communist Manifesto (Cambridge: Cambridge University Press, 1960), chaps. iii and iv.

42. Cf. J. J. Spengler, "Mercantilist and Physiocratic
Growth Theory, " Theories of Economic Growth, B. F. Hoselitz
et al. (Homewood: The Free Press, 1960), p. 4; also G. M.
Meier and R. E. Baldwin, Economic Development: Theory,
History, and Policy (New York: J. Wiley & Sons, 1957), p.
148.

43. Cf. Arthur Birnie, An Economic History of Europe
(1760-1939) (London: Methuen & Co. , 1957), p. 1; also, A. J.
Toynbee, Civilization on Trial (New York: Oxford University
Press, 1948), p. 8.

44. Adam Smith, The Wealth of Nations (Homewood, Ill.:
R. D. Irwin, Inc., 1963), I, 11.

45. See The Encyclopaedia Britannica (Chicago: Encyclopaedia Britannica, Inc., 1939), IV, 166-68.

46. Cf. K. E. Boulding, "The Economics of Knowledge
and the Knowledge of Economics," American Economic Review: Papers and Proceedings, LVI, 2 (May, 1966), 5.

47. Cf. Carl Polanyi, The Great Transformation: The
Political and Economic Origins of Our Time (Boston: Beacon
Press, 1962), pp. 43-47.

48. Rostow, op. cit., p. 38.

49. See, for details, L. M. Becker, The Triumph of
American Capitalism (New York: Simon & Schuster, 1940),
chaps. vii and viii.

50. See Richard Hofstadter, The Age of Reform: From
Bryan to F. D. R. (New York: McGraw Hill, 1964), pp. 403-13.

51. See Thorstein Veblen, The Theory of the Leisure
Class (New York: Modern Library, 1931), chap. 4.

52. Rostow, op. cit., p. 38.

53. Cf. Hagen, op. cit., pp. 276-77.

54. See C. K. Yang, Chinese Communist Society: The
Family and the Village (Cambridge, Mass.: M. I. T. Press,
1965), chaps. i and ii.

55. Ibid., pp. 10-21.

56. Ibid., p. 137.

57. See Mark Mancall, "The Kiakhta Trade," C. D.
Cowan, ed., The Economic Development of China and Japan:
Studies in Economic and Political Economy (New York:
Frederick A. Praeger, Inc., 1964).

58. See C. A. Buss, Asia in the Modern World (New York:
The Macmillan Company, 1964), pp. 237-38.

36   BURMA AND PAKISTAN

59. Cf. W. A. Lewis, The Theory of Economic Growth (Homewood, Ill.: R. D. Irwin, Inc., 1955), pp. 24-25.

60. See A. W. Watts, The Way of Zen (New York: The American Library of World Literature, 1960), Part I.

61. See Theodore de Bary, ed., Sources of Japanese Traditions (New York: Columbia University Press, 1958), chap. xviii.

62. See Hugh T. Patrick, "Lessons for Underdeveloped Countries from the Japanese Experience of Economic Development," The Indian Economic Journal, IX (October, 1961), 159-62; see, also, Eijiro Honjo, The Social and Economic History of Japan (New York: Russell & Russell, Inc., 1965), chap. vi.

63. See C. D. Carus and C. L. McNichols, Japan: Its Resources and Industries (New York: Harper & Row, 1944), chap. i.

64. Ajit Dasgupta, "India's Cultural Values and Economic Development: A Comment," Economic Development and Cultural Change, XIII, 1, Part I (October, 1964).

65. Cf. Hagen, op. cit., chap. 11.

66. See J. S. Furnivall, Colonial Policy and Practice (New York: New York University Press, 1956), p. 307.

67. For a detailed account, see Mya Maung, "Cultural Values and Economic Changes in Burma," The Asian Survey, IV, 1 (March, 1964).

68. Ibid., p. 8.

CHAPTER **2** BURMA VERSUS
PAKISTAN:
DEVELOPMENT
PARADOXES

A cursory comparison of the physical, economic and
political conditions of Burma and Pakistan after their inde-
pendence--in 1948 and 1947, respectively--suggests that the
Burmese prospect for development was greater than that of
Pakistan. The actual economic performance of the two countries in the 1950s and 1960s, however, reversed this trend,
thereby "confounding the prophets."[1] Looking at the natural
factor endowments alone is, therefore, neither sufficient nor
valid to account for the relative achievements in development
between any two LDCs. Events in Pakistan seem to rigorously
confirm the fact that the economic phenomenon of poverty can
be overcome by following appropriate social and economic
policies, whereas what happened in Burma reinforces the belief that economic underdevelopment is not necessarily caused
by a paucity of natural resources. Both cases reveal that the
process of economic development largely involved factors other
than economic--particularly the sociocultural matrix of ideology, motivation, cultural receptivity and innovative propensities
of peoples or social groups.
   The relative success of Pakistan's nation-building and
development planning has been attributed, principally, to its
development strategy of liberalizing internal and external
trades and stimulating private greeds for public benefits.[2]
Though this interpretation is subject to debate and oversimpli-
fies the developmental process, one can agree with the implication that there is room for the private sector in planning for
development. This position, naturally, has not been maintained by Burmese nationalist socialist leaders, whose value-
rationality of socialism in the most recent proclamation of
"the Burmese Way to Socialism" has led to formal adoption
of the Sino-Soviet model of development and to a total denial
of the role of private enterprise. The roots and development
of economic liberalization in Pakistan and of socialization in

Burma cannot be explained by an oversimplified view of
private- versus public-oriented policies in affecting economic
change but rather by an analysis of the process of social conflict that makes a social system closed or open, historically.
I shall argue in later chapters that the relative historic openness of Pakistan accounts for its economic miracle, whereas
the reverse is true of Burma.

It might, perhaps, be argued that Burma and Pakistan
are so different in their sociopolitical, cultural and economic
situations that any comparative study of their experiences and
achievements in the area of development may be fruitless as
far as establishing general conclusions pertinent to the problem
and solution of economic underdevelopment. It is my contention
that these differences are superficial within the dynamics of
social conflict and economic change and that any pretechnological, traditional societies confront substantively similar
problems of social change and development, despite their
structural variations. If anything, it is, indeed, even more
useful and fascinating to analyze and assess the relative achieve
ments or failures in these two countries, because the physical
conditions natural to them seem to suggest outcomes other than
those that have actually taken place during their independence.

What is even more paradoxical is that social and economic
policies adopted by these countries do not reflect the Marxian
mode of production or the social structure. The more authoritarian and highly stratified social structure of Pakistan has
not suppressed acquisitiveness and innovation, while the supposedly egalitarian and individualistic social structure of
Burma has not engendered a congenial environment for the
adoption and development of capitalism. The crucial questions
to be asked in solving these paradoxes are: (a) Why does
economic liberalization in Pakistan lead to a better economic
performance than in Burma? (b) What are the roots of the
different models of economic development in the two countries?
(c) What makes the social propensity to innovate in Pakistan
greater than in Burma? Most significant of all, it must be
asked whether or not the case of Pakistan shatters the Weberian
theses of marginal cultural brokers and Protestant ethics, as
Papanek has argued. [3] For the purpose of this study, I shall
maintain that development paradoxes in Pakistan and Burma
are not a simple function of dismantling or tightening economic
and social controls by the state, but they are due to complex
social changes and conflicts.

A CONTRAST OF PHYSICAL
AND ECONOMIC CONDITIONS

Population Pressure

The most striking difference between Pakistan and Burma is the population pressure on available resources. Although the growth of population, taken by itself, does not indicate a negative potential for development, given a similar stage of economic development and state of technology between any two countries, the one with less population pressure would certainly possess a greater prospect for development. This, of course, is a pure physical assessment, without considering the fact that a greater population pressure can give rise to a greater input of human effort and stimulate the will to economize.

In any case, it is commonly observed that Burma is relatively affluent in basic necessities, with no sign of abject poverty like her giant neighbors, China and India. In relation to Pakistan, Burma has been less handicapped physically by not having to confront such gigantic problems as Malthusian population pressure, a shortage of foodstuffs, the near or below subsistence standard of living, a shortage of fertile land and natural resources and the kind of catastrophic famine that seems to have historically plagued the Indian subcontinent, including what is now Pakistan. Although Pakistan's area (364,737 square miles) is larger than that of any European country, except Russia, and about one and a half times larger than Burma's (262,000 square miles), the population of Pakistan had been recorded in the 1950s as the sixth largest in the world. In 1951, the population of Pakistan exceeded that of Burma by about four times and, in the 1960s, by nearly five times, as shown in Table 1.

The comparative rates of population growth in the two countries indicate that Burma's growth has not presented any serious strain on the natural resources and standard of living, whereas the opposite is true of Pakistan. Population growth in Pakistan has been among the fastest in the world, with an annual compound rate of well above 2 percent since independence. The problem of how to provide gainful employment to the rising tide of the working population and, at the same time, maintain a living standard above subsistence has always been the regular concern of the development planners in Pakistan.

It was estimated that population growth in Pakistan would

TABLE 1

Comparative Growth of Population,
Burma and Pakistan, 1951-68
(In Millions)

Year	Burma	Pakistan	Percentage Annual Growth Burma	Pakistan
1951	18.674	80.590		
			1.4	2.3
1961	21.527	98.880		
			2.1	2.6
1968	26.400	121.760		

Sources: United Nations, Demographic Yearbook 1953 (New York: U.N., 1953); United Nations, Demographic Yearbook 1962 (New York: U.N., 1962); Report to the People by the Union of Burma Revolutionary Council 1969-70 (Rangoon: Revolutionary Council Government, Central Press, 1969); and Pakistan Economic Survey 1968-69 (Islamabad: Ministry of Finance, 1969).

have reached 2.7 percent by the end of 1969-70; in fact, it grew at 2.7 percent during the latter half of the 1960s.[4] By contrast, from the 1930s until 1961, the Burmese population growth averaged less than 1.5 percent.* In fact, during 1953-60, the growth rate was only 1 percent.[5] A recent estimate does indicate, however, that the population of Burma has begun to grow at an accelerated rate of a little over 2 percent. This, of course, changes the outlook for the potential development of Burma in the future. Another estimate indicates that the population of Pakistan would double every

---

*Note the United Nations' (U.N.) figures for Pakistan are understated. The main reason is the exclusion of Jammu-Kashmir territory. It must also be noted that the slower rate of population growth in Burma is due, partially, to its higher infant mortality rate.

thirty-two years or so--representing an annual growth rate of
about 3 percent, or more than 4 million each year.[6] These
purely statistical data seem to suggest the Pakistani economy
must grow at a pace of one to one and one-half times greater
than that of Burma in order to achieve an equivalent performance in either maintaining or raising the per capita income.
Assuming the same improvement in health and sanitation
standards for both countries, the prospect for confronting the
population explosion is greater for Pakistan than it is for
Burma in the light of simple land-population ratios.[*]

Physically, Pakistan is a disjointed country, East and
West being separated by hundreds of miles and characterized
by different terrain, climate, soil, population density, natural
resources and topography. Unlike Burma, with its natural in-
land waterways, Pakistan confronts difficult problems of transportation and communication within each of its segments and
between the mountainous West and the deltic East. The ex-
tremity of climate, rocky terrain and barren soil of West
Pakistan account for its lower density of population. It is
nearly six times as large as East Pakistan, where most water
resources and naturally cultivated land can be found and, therefore, a greater number of Pakistanis. As of 1951, the average
densities of East and West Pakistan were given as 777 and 208
per square mile, respectively. The 1961 Census indicated the
densities as 979 and 138, respectively.[7]

Land-Labor Ratio

According to a ranking of countries with respect to the
amount of land that is suitable for, or under, cultivation,
Pakistan ranked among the lowest; Pakistan's value of 0.24
hectares per capita was about one-half of Burma's 0.44 hectares
per capita, while the world median was given as 0.49 hectares
per capita.[8] In terms of persons per hectare of cultivated land,
Burma falls within the range of 0-0.49, whereas Pakistan falls
within the range of 3.0 and plus.[9] From these figures, it is
quite obvious that the average size of land holding by a cultivator in Burma is substantially larger than in Pakistan. It
was also estimated that the wasted land that could be brought
under cultivation in Burma amounts to 19 million acres, an

---

[*]This also assumes that both economies grow at some
positive rate. In the light of recent economic performances
of Burma, such an assumption may be unwarranted.

area substantially larger than that being currently cultivated
and almost as large as the historically cultivated one. [10]

These data suggest that the physical limitations of available land in Pakistan, in relation to the size and growth of
population, are far greater than Burma's, although it by no
means indicates the greater use of land resources or the development of agriculture in Burma. During the independent
period, Burma has not been able to cultivate the land that was
utilized during the colonial period, let alone add fresh land for
cultivation. Pakistan, by comparison, has expanded the acre-
age of cultivation through extensive programs of irrigation.
Pakistan ranked much higher than Burma in the percentage of
land under cultivation; this was given as about one-fourth of
its total area, of which three-fourths was irrigated. The
figure for Burma was slightly over 12.5 percent in recent
years. [11] This may be due to the fact that the need to cultivate
more land is not so great in Burma, which has been historically considered as one of the rice bowls of Asia, with an
annual export surplus of rice equaling its domestic consumption.

Capital and Technology

Despite the phenomenal difference in land-labor ratio between the two countries, it would not be an exaggeration to
state that both of them suffer from a tremendous shortage of
capital. Probably the per capita shortage of capital in Pakistan
is much greater than in Burma. Although the pattern of technology may be similar for both countries, it is quite difficult
to assess the relative levels of technology and the industrial
base. If one conceives of technology as a simple matter of
artifacts, the two countries share a common pattern of production techniques, with labor-intensive methods of production.
If a more sophisticated and broader concept of technology
covering the sociocultural matrix of skills, management,
motivation and values is adopted, [12] the economic miracle of
Pakistan can only be explained by its greater social propensity
to innovate. With respect to textiles and jute, for instance,
Pakistan's technology may be deemed as superior to Burma
historically. It may, however, be assumed that the technological gap between Burma and Pakistan is not so great as
to lead to the conclusion that the former is handicapped by an
elementary state of technology in the strict sense of the term.

Stage of Economic Development

The contribution of industrial production to national output during the first decade of independence indicates that the
two countries were in a similar stage of economic development. Industrial output accounted for less than 10 percent of
national output in both countries, while agriculture accounted
for roughly 55 to 60 percent of the gross domestic product.
About 70 percent of the working population in Burma and
Pakistan are still cultivators, whereas about 10 percent of the
population are urban dwellers. Recent data indicate, however,
that both industrial production and the urbanization of Pakistan
have been increasing at a more rapid rate than those of Burma.
Yet, the initial structural parity between Burma and Pakistan
is identical, in that both are predominantly agricultural rural
economies with a heavy dependency on external trade. While
the Pakistani economy depends heavily upon the production and
export of two major cash crops, jute and cotton, the Burmese
economy is monoculturally oriented to the production and export of rice. Since more than two-thirds of their export
earnings are derived from these crops, both economies confront similar problems of foreign-exchange shortages and
fluctuations, due to fluctuations of world prices for primary
products and because their capacity to import foreign capital
is a direct function of their capacity to export. In summary,
Burma and Pakistan possess these common characteristics of
an underdeveloped economy: a low per capita income, low per
capita capital, heavy dependency on the production and export
of primary products, more than 60 percent of the working
population engaged in agriculture and a low state of technology.
As has been suggested, Burma is fortunate to be spared from
the problem of population pressure on available resources.

A CONTRAST OF ECONOMIC SYSTEMS

From the period of independence to the present, the
economic models of development adopted by the governments
of Pakistan and Burma have been different. They have differed with respect to such basic concepts as ideals, social
goals, predilection toward socialism, the spirit of anticapitalism, the use of market mechanisms for stimulating private incentives and reliance on external sources of capital and
technology. Formally, the Pakistani economic system has

been built upon the model of a mixed economy typical of the
Western world whereas the Burmese economy has been in-
crementally shaped into a planned socialist economy of the
Sino-Soviet type.

Actually, both economies were constructed with a heavy
emphasis on the role of the state in initiating and maintaining
the process of economic development. Structurally, the model
of planning and administrative machinery for implementing
development plans did not differ substantially in the two countries during the first decade of their independence. In terms
of evolution, the Pakistani economic system has undergone
considerable dismantling of state controls and liberalization
of both internal and external trade, while the Burmese economy
has traveled in the opposite direction.

The subscription to a welfare state with a heavy reliance
on the private sector has been quite persistent on the part of
the Pakistani political leadership, despite limited concretization
in the earlier period of independence. Similarly, the commitment of the Burmese political leadership to build a socialist
economy, with little or no room for private enterprise, has
also been quite persistent from the beginning of independence
up to the present time. The real process of liberalization of
state controls on trade and industry in Pakistan began in 1962
under the constitutional government of General Ayub Khan,
whereas the state monopoly of trade and industry has been
established in Burma, since 1962, under the military regime
of General Ne Win.

The first decade of independence in Pakistan and Burma
exhibits some parallel experiences and efforts in the building
of a modern nation. These include internal strife and disorder
following the liquidation of British colonial rule; social and
political factionalism leading to rigorous power struggles; an
ideological crisis in the national identification of social goals
and development; the ambitious drafting and launching of development plans through a complex network of governmental
boards, corporations and departments; the boom and crisis
of foreign exchange during and after the Korean War, which
led to revision of development plans; and frustration at the
failure of overly ambitious development schemes. Differences
in their developmental experiences are reflected in the frequency of changes in the political power structure and in leadership, the process of instituting or dismantling a parliamentary
democracy and the changes in economic policies and strategies
of development.

Pakistan witnessed the collapse of parliamentary

democracy earlier than Burma, with a turnover in political
leaders every two years or so between 1948 and 1958 after
the death of Quaid-i-Azam (Mohammed Ali Jinnah) in 1947.
Political power in Burma during the same period changed
hands only once after the death of General Aung San in 1947,
when the military caretaker government of General Ne Win
took over from the All Burma Anti-Fascist Peoples' Freedom
League (AFPFL) Government of U Nu in 1958 for a brief
eighteen-month period. This does not mean that Burma was
politically more stable than Pakistan during that period. For
behind the seeming calmness of Burmese political scenes,
there were social and political insurgents who loomed large
in the countryside. In fact, the problem of insurgency has
remained a constant factor of major setback in Burma's nation-
building. Neither the civilian government nor the present
military regime has been able to solve this problem, in spite
of the military indictment of the civilian government for having
failed to subdue the insurgency, which was given as one of the
crucial reasons for the military coup of 1962.

During the first decade of independence, the Pakistani and
Burmese economic systems, structured by the respective
civilian governments, did not differ in kind as model welfare
states. Both economically and politically, Pakistan and Burma
represented a mixed economy of capitalism and socialism under
a constitutional government. The Burmese economic system
relied more heavily on socialization measures than its Pakistani
counterpart; but both were run with centralized governmental
planning agencies and development corporations under such
development plans as the Two-Year Development Plan and
Pyidawtha Eight-Year Plan for Burma and the Six-Year Development Program and Five-Year Development plans for
Pakistan. The planning machinery of both countries was built
upon the foundation of colonial administrative institutions with
the help of foreign experts, mostly Western advisers. The
development philosophy of both countries seemed to be in line
with the theory of balanced growth and the thesis that public
investment in both industries of social overhead capital and of
directly productive activities is the key to economic development. The first decade of independence, therefore, may be
appropriately termed the era of large-scale state economic
ventures and controls for both countries.

The planning machinery for Pakistan was built directly
upon the institutional foundation of its colonial heritage and of
Western sources of technology. The colonial foundation for
planning for development in Pakistan began earlier than in

Burma; before the end of World War II, a Department of Planning and Development had been created by the government of British India. Industrial development projects prepared by that Department were carried over into the early period of independence.

In 1948, two governmental agencies--the Development Board and Planning Advisory Board--were created, enabling Pakistan to utilize the various projects of the Department. By 1950, planning machinery in Pakistan received extensive assistance from the Colombo Plan for Cooperative Development in South and Southeast Asia, which incorporated the Six-Year Development Program of Pakistan into its general development schemes.[13] The Harvard Advisory Group also played a prominent role in formulating and revising various development projects undertaken by the Pakistan governments.

Between 1948 and 1951, Burma was confronting a serious political crisis, which nearly cost the AFPFL Government of U Nu its power to minority insurgents. In 1948, a Two-Year Development Plan was drawn up, but it was not actually launched until the end of 1950, due to social and political unrest. The actual effort of planning in Burma began in 1951-52, when the government organized a massive program for development under the banner of "Toward a Pyidawtha," meaning, literally, the building of a glorious country of peace, prosperity and happiness. Burma, like Pakistan, initially relied heavily upon the technological advice of Western foreign experts, a group of Oxford economists, the U. N. experts and the American firm of Knappen Tippets, Abbet, and McCarthy Engineering Company, along with Robert Nathan Associates. This curious reliance of the Burmese political leadership on capitalist-oriented Western experts for building a socialist economy suggests both the type of socialism and the contradictory spirit of Burmese politics.[14]

Early Development Plans

The early development plans of both Pakistan and Burma had a common feature; i. e. , the giving of some formal attention to the role of the private sector and the stimulation of private incentives. Pakistan's First Five-Year Plan (1955-60) and Burma's Pyidawtha Plan (1952-60) attached specific importance to domestic saving, which the planners felt would be partially supplied by the private sector via the stimulation of private investments. In the First Five-Year Plan of Pakistan, total investment was envisaged as Rs. 10, 800 million, of which

Rs. 7, 500 million was to be undertaken by the public sector
and the remainder by the private sector. Similarly, Burma's
Pyidawtha Plan anticipated that, by 1959, the relative shares
of the public and the private sectors in the gross capital formation would be equal at K. 559 million each.[*] In terms of the
strategy of economic development, therefore, both Pakistan
and Burma formally--if not actually--allowed under their
civilian governments some room for the private sector in the
process of capital formation. As the Pyidawtha Plan professed,
"To some extent, the rate of rise in total expenditures will
depend upon the degree to which the Government creates an
environment favorable to private investment. "[15]

In actually implementing these plans and formulating
specific targets, however, the cause of the private sector
seemed to go by default in both countries.[16] As of 1959-60,
the share of the public sector in the gross investment of
Pakistan was Rs. 1, 370 million against Rs. 500 million of the
private sector, while, in Burma, the relative shares of the
public and private sectors were K. 580 million and K. 454
million, respectively,[17] far short of the anticipated target.
It seemed that development planning in Pakistan prior to 1958
relied more heavily upon governmental development expenditures than Burma in terms of actual capital formation. A
little more than 50 percent of the public development expenditures of Pakistan's First Five-Year Plan was financed through
external assistance from Western sources.[18]

Economic Role of the State

Development planning in both Pakistan and Burma during
their first decade of independence endorsed the balanced growth
theory on the one hand and the thesis that large-scale state
economic actions are not only necessary but also conducive
to the development of private incentives in saving and investment. With an identical attitude toward the economic role of
the state, Pakistan and Burma launched their respective development plans under a system of direct controls of both
internal and external sectors of the economies. The net effect
of large-scale inept state interference with the functioning of
the economy in both countries was the misallocation of

---

[*]The Burmese kyats (K.) and the Pakistani rupees (Rs.)
are directly comparable, in that they both have an almost
identical foreign exchange value--about K. 5 or Rs. 5 to
U. S. $1.

resources, sometimes in simple matters of price policy and
marketing of products. With respect to the disincentive effect
of large-scale state interference, M. Haq remarked that the
First Five-Year Plan of Pakistan had produced an economic
environment in which "creative energies of an otherwise
dynamic private sector were chained rather than unleashed."[19]
The same observation may be made as to the net effect of the
Pyidawtha Plan on Burma. In the field of social services as
in agriculture, the Pyidawtha Government of Burma employed
massive state interference and aid programs in introducing
what was popularly known as "the mass movement." From
mass education to the mass cooperative movement, the principle of optimum allocation of resources was abandoned in
favor of the big push on all fronts by the government.

One example of inefficiency due to inept state control,
cited by a Burmese economist, was the uniform price policy
of the State Agricultural Marketing Board (SAMB) of the govern
ment of the Union of Burma in the purchase of rice through its
numerous buying depots. The policy was adopted in the name
of socialism by offering a uniform price for the whole year and
to all cultivators of different geographic regions.* Such an inept state action not only preempted the stabilization function of
speculation but also produced a disincentive effect and economi
waste by flooding the government's warehouses with rice.[20]
Hla Myint, attributing the cause of this to the wrong image of
economic development and the strategy of planning, made the
following observation:

> Many economists visiting Burma during this period
> characteristically overlooked this "simple" but ex-
> tremely wasteful misallocation of resources in their
> preoccupation with the more elaborate development
> plans, including the expansion of investment in
> "infrastructure."[21]

This view is a bit overstated with respect to the total
process of development, which not only entails enforcement

---

*As Everett E. Hagety commented on the first draft of
this study, this egalitarian policy, while in effect subsidizing
growers far from port or penalizing those close to port, would
not have been disastrous if competently administered. Indeed,
one of the major problems of development planning in the
LDCs is the inability to administer or implement the plans
adopted.

of the so-called simple principles of economics but also comprehension of the social and political motivation of those who initiate, and those who respond to, certain economic actions. Yet, it is quite true that one of the major developmental dilemmas of a newly independent nation has been the problem of reconciliation between the goals of equity and efficiency, on the one hand, and the reconciliation between the highly complex and often inefficient large-scale state economic actions and the simple and efficient market mechanisms, on the other. The problem is more acute for a country like Burma, whose political and cultural aversion to the economic institutions of capitalism has been a persistent trait of its overall development goals and planning.

A CONTRAST OF ECONOMIC GROWTH

Given the natural physical conditions, the economic performance of Pakistan and Burma since their independence has been quite contrary to the expectation of many observers. The gloomy prospect of Pakistan's future--and the bright prospect of Burma--have been turned around dramatically in recent years. It is tempting to attribute this paradox to different social and political problems confronting the two countries at the time of independence. Perhaps, modernization problems in Burma have been more difficult than Pakistan's. Yet, at the very outset of development planning, Pakistan's social and political problems were no less difficult and demanding than those of Burma. (I will explain them in detail in the next chapter. At present, it is sufficient to point out that both countries confronted similar problems: a lack of able administrators, of political stability and stable governments, of social solidarity and of bases for democratization.)

Despite the fact that the Indian subcontinent was spared from the devastating effects of World War II, Pakistan after the partition confronted armed conflict within and without its borders, along with colossal problems of socioeconomic dislocations of thousands of refugees and unification of multiple ethnic and political groups. The very size of Pakistan, its social pluralism and its disjointed segments are enough to indicate that it was not socially and politically less handicapped than Burma in modernization and nation-building.

Rates of Growth

The general pattern of economic growth in the 1950s and
1960s may be described as a transition from stagnation to
accelerated growth for Pakistan and from sustained growth
to depression for Burma. In terms of both total and per
capita rates of growth of output, the economic performance
of Burma under the Two-Year Development Plan (1950-52)
and the Pyidawtha Plan and its revision, the Four-Year Plan
(1956-60), was better than Pakistan's under the Six-Year Development Program (1950-56) and the First Five-Year Plan.
According to the United Nations' 1966 Statistical Yearbook,
the growth rates of the Burmese[*] and Pakistani economies
were recorded as 6.3 percent and 2.7 percent, respectively,
with respect to the "average annual rates of real gross domes
tic product at factor cost" in the 1950s.[22] In per capita term
these represented 4.3 percent and 0.6 percent, respectively.
   It should be noted that the superior performance of the
Burmese economy over the Pakistan economy in the 1950s
was largely due to its very low level of output, relating to its
prewar level. The gross domestic product (GDP) of Burma
in 1949-50[24] was about 70 percent of the prewar level (1938-
39), indicating that Burma's major problems of development
were mainly reconstruction and rehabilitation of the War-
damaged economy.[25] In this sense, Burma's economic growt
in the 1950s is not actually a process of growth but of reestab
lishing a past standard of performance; Pakistan did not have
such a precedent, unless one thinks in terms of India's economic history.
   The growth of the GDP of Burma between 1950 and 1960
was roughly 77 percent, while it was only 28 percent for
Pakistan.[**] Of course, the per capita GDPs growth in Burm

-----

[*]The Burmese official data were usually given at 1947-48
prices and current prices. The planners (K.T.A. group),
however, employed 1950-51 prices. I have ventured, for a
comparative purpose, to adjust the Burmese figures to 1959-
60 prices by estimating the deflator as .935. Cf. L. J.
Walinsky, Economic Development of Burma (1951-60) (New
York: The Twentieth Century Fund, 1962), p. 357. See, als
his footnote on page 356, where his complaint was lodged
against the faulty techniques of price-transformation of the
Burmese Government, although he himself did not clearly
indicate his deflator.
   [**]The GDPs of Burma and Pakistan were in terms of
their respective currencies.

TABLE 2

Comparative Growth of Gross Domestic Product,
Burma and Pakistan, 1949-60[a]
(In Billions)

Country	Gross Domestic Product (GDP)	1949-50	1959-60	Percentage Annual Growth 1949-60
Burma	GDP	K. 3. 390	K. 5. 911	5. 9
	Per Capita GDP	K. 183	K. 290	4. 7
Pakistan	GDP	Rs. 24. 960	Rs. 32. 340	2. 4
	Per Capita GDP	Rs. 316	Rs. 327	0. 3

[a] The data are in 1959-60 prices.

Source: United Nations Statistical Yearbooks, Government of Burma Economic Surveys, and Government of Pakistan Economic Surveys, 1951-1961.

looked even more impressive. The agricultural and industrial origins of Burma's GDP were recorded as 40 percent and 8 percent in 1950 and as 32 percent and 15 percent in 1960. The Pakistani counterparts were 58 percent and 8 percent in 1950 and 53 percent and 10 percent in 1960. These figures seem to indicate further that the Pakistani economy in the 1950s did not possess a larger industrial base for development than Burma. It is also interesting to note that these developments took place in Burma and Pakistan in spite of differences in priority as to the allocation of development expenditures to the agricultural and industrial sectors of the economies. It has been charged that one of the failures of development planning in Pakistan in the 1950s, for example, was neglect of the agricultural sector,[26] while Burmese planners have been credited with their effort to give priority to the agricultural sector.

Balance of Payments

The balance of payments for Pakistan and Burma reflected fluctuations in the prices of their major crops--rice for Burma

and jute and cotton for Pakistan. Both countries enjoyed favor
able conditions up to 1953 from a post-War, and later the
Korean, economic boom. These created high hopes for financ
ing development expenditures, particularly in Burma when the
Pyidawtha Plan was launched--hopes that were shattered by
the end of 1953, when development planners in Burma had to
revise their initial assumptions and ex-ante targets.

The year 1953-54 should have driven home to the Burmese
Government and its planning advisers that successful planning
hinged upon favorable terms of trade and the volume of rice
exports more than any other factors. A deficit of payments
amounting to K. 94 million in 1953-54, for instance, was incurred primarily because of the decline in the total value of
rice exports from K. 1 billion in 1952-53 to K. 840 million in
1953-54.[27] The price of rice fell sharply in 1953-54. The
government's refusal to sell rice at depressed world prices
caused a large stock of unsold rice to accumulate. Burma
fared badly in the bilateral barter trade ageements entered,
especially with the Sino-Soviet Bloc.[28] As a result, foreign
exchange reserves dwindled rapidly from K. 1.186 billion in
1952-53 to K. 510 million by the end of 1955; they were never
restored to the level of 1952-53. The highest level of foreign
exchange reserves regained during the latter half of the 1950s
was K. 785 million in 1958-59.[29]

With respect to the balance of trade, the latter part of the
Pyidawtha period suffered from three years of deficit, 1957
being the worst year, with a deficit of about K. 320 million.
In 1960, a deficit of K. 203 million occurred to end the Pyidawt
period. Despite these unfavorable developments in external
trade, the Burmese economy throughout the Pyidawtha era
managed to export annually over K. 1 billion every year except
1958. Even in 1958, the value of exports was more than K. 900
million.[30] The average annual volume of rice exports, for
example, was between 1 million and 1.5 million tons, indicatin
sustained growth in the production and export of the major cro
However, the export of rice has remained below 50 percent of
its 1938-39 level throughout the independent period.

External trade in the Pakistani economy suffered from
similar fluctuations; the balance of trade and foreign exchange
reserves reflected the post-War and Korean highs, followed by
a slump, with deficits greater in amount and of longer duration
than in Burma. During the 1952-60 period, for instance,
Pakistan incurred a yearly deficit in the balance of trade, except for the years 1953, 1954 and 1955. Deficits in 1953 and
1960 amounted to over Rs. 1 billion each. Taking 1953 as the

base year, the annual volume of cotton and jute exports remained below that peak year for the entire span of the 1950-60
decade; the lowest year was 1959, when Pakistan could export
only one-half of the volume of 1953.[31] Foreign exchange reserves in Pakistan, like Burma, depleted at a rapid rate after
the Korean boom, and, by 1955, the foreign exchange surplus
accumulated during the boom period was said to have been
completely depleted.[32] In absolute terms, however, foreign
exchange reserves in Pakistan did not fluctuate as severely
as those of Burma, remaining well above Rs. 200 million
throughout the 1952-60 period. This differential may be attributed to Pakistan's import austerity programs; more significantly, it was due to the relatively large amount of external
financing, such as public grants and loans (particularly from
the United States), private investments and other capital in-
flows. With regard to the importance of foreign capital, G.
Papanek remarked: "With declining export earnings and increasing demand for imports, and with exchange reserves
used up, the economy continued to function and develop only
because inflow of foreign resources rose substantially."[33]

Foreign Assistance

The percentage of foreign assistance in the gross national
product (GNP) of Pakistan, for example, rose from 0.2 in
1949-50 to 4.7 in 1959-60; in total investment, the percentage
rose from 3.2 to 44.7 during the same period.[34] The average
annual value of foreign assistance was about $10 million in the
early 1950s; in the late 1950s and up to the mid-1960s, it was
over $650 million. Comparable figures for Burma are not
available, though it may be assumed that there was less reliance on foreign assistance for financing development than
in Pakistan. This does not mean, of course, that Burmese
development expenditures were financed primarily by domestic
sources; one estimate indicates that during the Pyidawtha
Plan's period, nearly one-third of all public expenditures were
financed by foreign aid.[35] However, the functioning and sustained development of the Burmese economy in the 1950s was
not due to the continual and substantial inflow of foreign resources to the degree that it was in the case of Pakistan.
In fact, economic nationalism and mistrust of foreign capital,
particularly from the Western world, have been one of the
major obstacles to the process of development planning in
Burma. The history of American foreign aid to Burma testifies
most lucidly to that fact.

Comparative Evaluation of Economic Growth

The 1950s

The superior performance of the Burmese, as opposed
to the Pakistani, economy in the 1950s was due to a number
of reasons, chief of which were Pakistan's natural physical
handicaps and its lack of a stable government. Some of
Pakistan's physical limitations have been mentioned previously
they were augmented by the social and political chaos following
partition. The frequency of changes in the political power
structure of Pakistan, plus the misallocation of resources due
to large-scale inept state actions, had hindered Pakistan from
launching a national development plan until the mid-1950s. [36]
Despite this slowness in development planning, the relative
achievements of the Pyidawtha Plan and the First Five-Year
Plan seemed to be identical--both plans achieved 80 percent
of their targets. The Pyidawtha Plan reached 80 percent of
its objective of K. 7 billion GDP by the end of 1960, as the
actual GDP in 1950-51 prices was K. 5. 6 billion. Similarly,
the actual national income of Pakistan in 1959-60 was Rs. 29. 5
billion instead of the planned target figure of Rs. 30. 015, or
an actual increase of 12 percent rather than the planned increase of 15 percent at the end of 1960. [37]
In a comparative evaluation of economic growth between
Pakistan and India, E. S. Mason gave two major reasons for
the relatively poor performance of the Pakistani economy in
the 1950s: (a) poorly supplied resources and (b) lack of a stable
government, which could manage an unstable country. [38] These
same two reasons may be applied to the relative performance
of the Burmese and Pakistani economies. Mason added further
that giving a broad meaning to the term "management," the
Pakistani economy in the 1950s, as well as in the 1960s, was
poorly managed relative to India. The efficiency of management of the Burmese economy by the Pyidawtha Government
cannot be judged as higher.
The year 1958 seemed to be a critical year for both
Pakistan and Burma politically, if not economically; it marked
the end of the civilian era of government for the former, the
beginning of the rise of a military elite on the political scene
for the latter. It was, also, the year of what is termed "the
cleanup" and management of the economy by the eighteen-
month military regime in Burma. The year 1962 was also an
important year for both countries in their reconstitution of
parliamentary democracy and the extensive dismantling of

state controls in Pakistan by the government of President Ayub Khan. For Burma, it marked the end of more than a decade of experimenting with a parliamentary system of government under civilian political leadership and the ushering in of an era of military rule by the Revolutionary Council Government of General Ne Win, along with measures of total nationalization under the banner of "the Burmese Way to Socialism."

Incidentally, a liberal attitude toward private enterprise and investments--both domestic and foreign--began to appear in the official policies of the Burmese government by the mid-1950s. In the Four-Year Plan, the government indicated its willingness to transfer certain non-key industries to the private sector, to establish an investment law to stimulate foreign and domestic investments, and to take other measures to reduce state economic activities. [39] In 1959, an Investment Act was passed, reflecting the change in economic policy, though its implementation was never really concretized, due to the rapid deterioration of political conditions following the return of U Nu to political power in 1960. Since 1962, the development strategy of Pakistan and Burma has traveled in opposite directions, reversing the pattern of growth that took place in the 1950s.

The 1960s

The relative economic growth of Pakistan and Burma in the 1960s may be best described, to use G. Papanek's phrase, as "confounding the prophets." [40] The dismal and gloomy picture of a country such as Pakistan with its colossal problems of physical handicaps, Malthusian population pressure, and sociopolitical turmoil seemed to change quite astonishingly into a bright picture of potential growth, judging by economic performance in the 1960s. By the same token, a country like Burma, with relatively fortunate factor endowments and a natural affluence in basic necessities, has suddenly found itself in the midst of an economic crisis unparalleled in its entire history--a crisis in which rice shortages and black-marketeering have become common news. To the amazement of outside observers, the economic growth of Pakistan in the 1960s has been quite impressive, while the economic depression of Burma has been equally spectacular, not only to outside observers but also to the Burmese, including the military rulers themselves. (So far, the economic growth of Pakistan is not in the same class with that of Japan and West Germany during the post-World War II period; yet, in the light of its historic

abject poverty and famine, its growth must be rated as a rare
achievement of the evolutionary approach to economic development.)

The rate of economic growth of Pakistan between 1961 and
1968, relative to that of the 1950s, represents an increase of
more than 250 percent in the total and 1, 000 percent in the per
capita rates of growth. By the mid-1960s, Pakistan attained
self-sufficiency in foodstuffs and, thereby, met the population
pressure on the living standard. In contrast, the economic
performance of Burma deteriorated drastically in the 1960s,
with a number of years actually showing a decline in output.
Taking 1964-65 as the base year, Burma's GDP has remained
below 100 in every consecutive year, except the estimated GDP
of 1968-69. [41] The decline of output took place during 1963-64,
1965-66 and 1966-67, indicating an average negative rate of
growth.

Industrial production in Pakistan in the 1960s has shown
a phenomenal increase of 234 percent above the 1958 level,
and the annual rate of growth of manufacturing production was
given as more than 14 percent. [42] In contrast, Burma's industrial production was reported to have declined in both the
public and private sectors. [43] The industrial origin of Pakistan
GDP in the 1960s has increased to 12 percent, while it may
be safely assumed that Burma's industrial production and its
contribution to the GDP has been stagnant in recent years. With
respect to agricultural production, an index indicated that, by
the end of 1965, both Pakistan and Burma produced about 20
percent above the level of 1961, the annual growth rate of
Pakistan being much higher than that of Burma. Since 1960,
Pakistan's most impressive performance is in agricultural
production, which has been growing at an annual rate of 4. 1
percent, or nearly four times greater than that of the 1950s. [44]
Agricultural production in Burma, on the other hand, has shown
a drastic deterioration, due to a combination of factors, among
which military mismanagement and crop failures are quite
conspicuous. In comparison to the peak year of 1959, for instance, with an output of 7. 027 million metric tons of rice, in
1964, the highest production year in the 1960s, Burma's rice
production was above the 1959 level only by about 1. 5 million
tons. [45] With a higher rate of population growth in the 1960s,
Burma's stagnant agricultural production has been, and will be
the major problem of development.

In the balance of trade for Pakistan and Burma, external
trade in the 1960s shows a similar pattern of continual deficit,
but with different causes. Pakistan's trade balance deficit

TABLE 3

Comparative Growth of Gross Domestic Product,
Burma and Pakistan, 1961-68[a]
(In Billions)

Country	Gross Domestic Product (GDP)	1961-62	1967-68	Percentage Annual Growth 1962-68
Burma	GDP	K. 6. 378	K. 7. 961	0. 40
	Per Capita GDP	K. 274	K. 302	0. 15
Pakistan	GDP	Rs. 35. 079	Rs. 48. 526	5. 60
	Per Capita GDP	Rs. 337	Rs. 399	3. 00

[a] Burmese data are in 1964-65 prices; the Pakistani data are in 1959-60 prices.

Sources: Report to the People by the Union of Burma Revolutionary Council 1969-70 (Rangoon: Revolutionary Council Government, Central Press, 1969); Pakistan Economic Survey 1968-69 (Islamabad: Ministry of Finance, 1969).

TABLE 4

Comparative Patterns of Foreign Trade,
Burma and Pakistan, 1961-68[a]
(In Billions)

Country	Trade	1961-62	1964-65	1967-68
Burma	Exports	K. 1. 2617	K. 1. 0788	K. . 5176
	Imports	K. 1. 0436	K. 1. 4129	K. . 7147
Pakistan	Exports	Rs. 1. 7864	Rs. 2. 3954	Rs. 3. 0700
	Imports	Rs. 3. 1876	Rs. 5. 3742	Rs. 4. 6547

[a] The data are at constant prices. Burmese data are in 1964-65 prices; Pakistani data are in 1959-60 prices.

Sources: Report to the People by the Union of Burma Revolutionary Council 1969-70 (Rangoon: Revolutionary Council Government, Central Press, 1969) pp. 16-17; Pakistan Economic Survey 1968-69 (Islamabad: Ministry of Finance, 1969), Appendix, p. 90.

arises not from a decline in major exports but from a continual increase in the import of capital goods, commodity aid
under the Public Law (PL) 480 program and invisibles. By
contrast, Burma's deficit in trade and balance of payments
can be traced, almost entirely, to the continuous decline of
exports since 1962--rice, in particular--in spite of very
strong measures of import controls exercised by the government.

    In 1967-68, the value of Burma's exports declined to less
than one-half of the 1961-62 level, while, in Pakistan, the
value of exports increased to more than one and one-half times
those of 1967-68. It should be noted further that, since 1962,
Burma's exports have declined every year, while Pakistan's
have increased. Similarly, the capacity to import has been
severely reduced for Burma.

    The single most important cause of Burma's trade deficit
has been the steady decline of rice exports. Again, taking
1962 as the base year, the index of the volume of rice exports
has shown a monotonously declining trend, reaching its lowest
level--30 percent of 1962--in 1967-68. [46] The average annual
export of rice since 1962 has been less than 500,000 metric
tons, amounting to less than 60 percent of the 1962 level and
less than 50 percent of the average level in the 1950s. The
decline has been more drastic since 1964-65, averaging about
15 percent, or an average export level of only about 300,000
tons. (Burmese economists estimated that, at this rate of
decline, rice exports would reach a zero level by 1970.)[47]
Since 1964, the export of teak, also, has been declining.

    Pakistan's exports, however, have steadily grown in term
of both value and volume since 1960, reaching their highest
value (over Rs. 3 billion) in 1967-68. Taking the same base
year, the volume of cotton exported in 1967-68 has been nearly
200 percent greater, though jute exports declined by some 30
percent for the same year. The foreign exchange reserves
of Pakistan also increased in the early 1960s, though, in recent years, they have shown a decrease, due primarily to
increased imports for development and the reduced rate of
foreign aid.

    In Burma, there was a sharp increase of foreign exchange
reserves in the years immediately following the military take-
over, due to large-scale state control of trade and nationalization of all foreign and domestic enterprises. These, too,
have declined drastically in recent years, despite strong
measures of direct controls on imports along with the decline
of rice exports; as of 1967-68, the foreign exchange reserves

of Burma were listed at K.71.2 million, less than the average
level of the late 1950s.

In spite of the vociferous proclamation of the intention of
building a socialist economy of "the planned, proportional
development of all the national productive forces" via measures
of nationalization and ownership of all national means of production by the state, cooperatives and collective unions, [48]
the only thing that has been accomplished today by the military
junta of Burma is in the nationalization of the economy. There
has not been any economic plan for development, and the modus
operandi of the development agencies has largely remained the
same, except for such things as changes in names (People's
Stores Corporation, and so forth).

Without any significant structural changes, the administrative machinery and functional control of the Burmese economy
remains centrally organized through twenty-two corporations
and their branches. The state-owned corporations, governmental councils, committees and stores overrun the entire
economy, thereby displacing private enterprise and dispensing
with the market mechanism in the production, consumption
and distribution of goods and services.

Within this pattern, the process of decision-making is now
controlled by a hierarchy of military authorities, set up on
the basis of former political divisions and ministries. These
military wungyis, or ministers, are the nucleus members of
the Burma Socialist Program Party (BSPP), in charge of the
functioning of certain sectors of the economy. For example,
in instituting a system of state capitalization the Ministry of
Commerce and Development has taken over the responsibility
for internal trade and the distribution of rationed goods and
services through the People's Stores Corporation, as well as
external trade through the Myama Export and Import Corporation. Essentially, therefore, the twenty-two corporations are
de facto former governmental development agencies, simply
renamed and put under the direct command of the ministers
and special duty officers.

Thus, the socialist economy of the present Revolutionary
Council Government, under its official philosophy of the
Burmese Way to Socialism, simulates a command economy
only in the state's ownership of the means of production; it
has no real machinery for planning and no systematic method
for creating the so-called socialist economy of "planned proportional development."[49] The only planning agency that
exists in name has been the Socialist Economy Planning Committee of the BSPP Party, which came into existence only

after 1965. Economic planning in Burma since 1962 must, therefore, be recorded as nonexistent; the functioning of the economy has, rather, been based on former development agencies, with a greater degree of centralism in the process of decision-making and control. That is to say, the socialist economy of Burma today is run by new military management, with massive direct controls in substituting state enterprises for private ones.

The Pakistani economy, however, has been operating along the lines of two consecutive development plans since the end of the First Five-Year Plan in 1960. Unlike Burma, the economy of Pakistan has not suffered any disruptions or drastic alterations in the process of planning, except for significant changes in the policies and strategies of development. This may be one of the reasons for Pakistan's better economic performance in the 1960s.

The Second Five-Year Plan (1960-65) was drawn up in 1958 by the Martial Law Government of General Ayub Khan and was launched in 1960 with a different philosophy and approach regarding sectoral priority in the allocation of resource and development expenditures.

The achievements of the Second Plan, after a careful revision of its targets in 1961, were quite impressive: they exceeded the projected or ex-ante targets with respect to both absolute change and rate of growth of total and per capita output. The actual increase of the GNP during the planned period was about 24 percent,[*] against the initial projected increase of 20 percent, and the actual rate of growth of the real GNP was 4.8 percent, as compared with the rate of growth of 2.4 percent achieved during the First Five-Year Plan. The rate of growth of per capita income was 2 percent, in contrast to the near zero rate in the 1950s.[50]

The major breakthrough occurred in the rate of capital formation, which increased from 10 percent in 1959-60 to 20 percent in 1964-65, with almost 50 percent of the gross investment financed from foreign sources.[51] The relative share of public and private sectors in investment showed an increase of 5 percent for the public sector during the Second Plan, or 55 percent, compared with 50 percent for the First Plan. It should be noted that the planned target for the private share was much less than the actual 45 percent achieved, which

---

[*]The revised estimate of increase in GNP was 24 percent. It seems, therefore, that the Second Plan's achievement of its absolute target was 100 percent.

suggests the successful stimulation of private incentives in investment by the government. The average annual rate of saving also increased sharply, from 4.8 percent in the 1950s to 9.5 percent during the Second Plan. [52]

The impressive achievements of the Second Five-Year Plan relative to the First, as well as the entire economic performance of Pakistan in the 1950s and Burma in the 1960s, were due to a number of factors--the most conspicuous among which were the restoration of political stability in 1958 and the major shift of economic policies toward indirect controls of the economy. Since 1958, economic policy and development have proceeded with the definite objective of creating an environment that would stimulate private incentives and enterprises. Programs such as Land Reform, Village AID, the Tax Holiday, the Export Bonus Scheme and an Investment Promotion Bureau were initiated in Pakistan soon after the military takeover in 1958. With such agencies as the Pakistan Industrial Development Corporation and the Pakistan Industrial Finance Corporation serving as the Industrial Development Bank, the government of General Ayub Khan proceeded with a basic policy of stimulating economic activities in the private sector in the belief "that the implementation of the programme of industrial development will depend primarily upon the private sector."[53] This philosophy was put into practice with improvement measures in the machinery of planning and coordination under a system of basic democracies, in which the Pakistani were given the opportunity of direct participation in the process of sociopolitical and economic change.

To be sure, the economic achievements of Pakistan in the 1960s cannot simply be attributed to domestic measures of the liberalization of trade and industry or to the adoption of a free-enterprise economic system as such, since it is the state that has the pragmatic outlook and takes the initiative in the process of economic development. It can be ascertained, however, that, since 1958, the role of the state in Pakistan has been more oriented to the use of the market-mechanism and the stimulation of private incentives in the building of a modern industrial nation than it has in Burma. Most important of all, the government of Pakistan has consistently paid attention to the external sector of the economy and, particularly, to foreign sources of capital and technology.

Even though it will be extremely difficult to determine to what extent the economic growth of Pakistan in the 1960s is due to the incessant inflow of foreign capital and technology, it is more than apparent that, without external aid, Pakistan's

task of developing its economy would have been monumental.
The public rate of capital formation, as well as the source of
development expenditures in Pakistan, have depended upon
foreign aid, loans and investments; hence, the important role
of external financing in development planning. In 1959-60,
for example, external resources made up 4.3 percent of the
GNP, compared with 7.1 percent in 1964-65. The annual inflow of foreign capital averaged about Rs.1 billion in the late
1950s and about Rs.2 billion in the 1960s, reaching its peak
of over Rs.2.6 billion in 1964-65. [54] The crucial role played
by foreign aid in the Second Five-Year Plan was clearly demon
strated in the field of agriculture, where the goal of self-
sufficiency in foodstuffs was attained through an increase in
the allocation of development expenditures to the agricultural
sector (24 percent of total investment, compared with 10 percent of the First Plan), and a sizeable import of food grains
under the PL 480 commodity aid program.

Not to undermine the role of domestic financing in agricultural development, it should be noted that certain measures
helped to stimulate private incentives and enterprise in both
agriculture and industry. These include Land Reform (1958),
by which the traditional landholding system (jagirs) was abolished and the redistribution of land accomplished, thereby
giving incentives of private ownership and investment to small
farmers; the lifting of price control on marketing of agricultur
al products; the Export Bonus Scheme (1959); and the Export
Credit Guarantee (1962). The substantial inflow of commodity
aid in agriculture mitigated the shortage of foreign exchange
and capital and relieved the pressure of population on the living
standard, thereby providing greater capital and opportunity to
devote to industrial development. [55]

With the ostensible accomplishments of the Second Plan
coming to an end in 1965, the government of Pakistan launched
a Third Five-Year Plan, with even higher targets of economic
growth. The long-term objectives of the Plan included the
following: (a) the tripling of the GNP from about Rs.44 billion
in 1965 to about Rs.145 billion in 1985, (b) provision of full
employment, (c) parity in per capita income between East and
West Pakistan, (d) universal literacy, and (e) the elimination
of dependency on foreign aid. [56] The immediate objectives of
the Plan included: (a) a 30 percent increase in the GNP by the
end of 1970, or an annual rate of growth of 5.4 percent, in
order to increase total investment by 53 percent over the
five-year period, (b) the reduction of disparity of income for
various regions, (c) the provision of 4.5 million new jobs,

(d) the strengthening of the balance of payments and foreign exchange to reach a level of Rs. 4. 250 billion by 1970, (e) the arrest of population growth, and (f) other improvements in social welfare. [57] As to the sectoral allocation of development expenditures and capital formation, the government was expected to take on the greater share in the agricultural sector, while private enterprise remained responsible for the industrial sector.

The strategy of the Third Five-Year Plan was distinctly directed toward building a welfare state, with explicit emphasis on planning through the market mechanism and stimulation of private enterprise. Changes in emphasis and the priority of targets took place mainly in the fields of agriculture--allotting Rs. 1. 860 billion, compared with Rs. 0. 8 billion of the Second Plan, the large-scale industries and the goal of self-sufficiency in the basic industries through the policy of export-oriented industrialization. In the development of private industries, the role of the public sector under the Third Plan has been relatively greater than that of the Second Plan, due to greater emphasis on the correction of regional disparities in economic growth. [58]

From all available indicators, it may be concluded that the targets of the Third Plan are more than likely to be realized--and that the results could be even more impressive than those of the Second Plan. Since 1965, the growth of the GNP has been consistently higher than during the previous Five-Year Plan; i. e., 5 percent in 1966-67 and 8. 3 percent in 1967-68. The average rate of growth for the first three years of the Plan was recorded at 6 percent; the phenomenal growth of agricultural production that has taken place since 1967-68 may be taken as an indicator of the possibility of an annual average growth rate of the GNP of about 6. 5 percent for the entire five-year period. [59] These unprecedented rates of growth in both the agricultural and industrial sectors during 1967-68 overcame the relatively poor performances, due, primarily, to bad harvests of the Pakistani economy, in the first two years of the Plan.

NOTES

1. Gustav Papanek, Pakistan's Development: Social Goals and Private Incentives (Cambridge, Mass.: Harvard University Press, 1967).

2. Papanek, ibid. chap. viii.

3. Papanek, ibid., pp. 46-55.

4. See Ministry of Finance, Pakistan Economic Survey 1968-69 (Islamabad: Ministry of Finance, 1969), Appendix, p. 2.

5. United Nations, Demographic Yearbook 1961 (New York: U.N., 1961), p. 110.

6. See A. M. Ghouse, "The Economy of Pakistan," A. M. Ghouse, ed., Studies in Economic Development: With Special Reference to Pakistan (Lahore: The Businessmen Seminar, 1962), p. 27.

7. See, for details, J. R. Andrus and A. F. Mohammed, The Economy of Pakistan (Stanford, Calif.: Stanford Universit Press, 1958). The United Nations' Demographic Yearbook 1967 (New York: U.N., 1968), gave the densities of Burma and Pakistan as 38 and 113, respectively.

8. N. S. Ginsburg, Atlas of Economic Development (Chicago: University of Chicago Press, 1961), p. 46.

9. E. E. Hagen, The Economics of Development (Homewood, Ill.: R. D. Irwin, Inc., 1968), p. 19.

10. W. S. Woytinsky and E. S. Woytinsky, World Population and Production: Trend and Outlook (New York: The Twentieth Century Fund, 1953), p. 354; also, Season and Crop Report 1941 (Rangoon: Government Printing and Stationery Office, 1941), pp. 22-23.

11. Ginsburg, op. cit., p. 50.

12. See J. J. Murphy, "Retrospect and Prospect," D. L. Spencer and A. Woronniak, eds., The Transfer of Technology to Developing Countries (New York: Frederick A. Praeger, Inc., 1967), pp. 6-9.

13. See, for details, Albert Waterson, Planning in Pakistan (Baltimore: The Johns Hopkins Press, 1963), chap. iii.

14. For its analysis, see Mya Maung, "Socialism and Economic Development of Burma," Asian Survey, IV, 12 (December, 1964).

15. Knappen, Tippets, Abbet, and McCarthy Engineering Co., Comprehensive Report: Economic and Engineering Development of Burma (London: Hazel Watson & Viney, Ltd., 1953), I, 40.

16. Cf. Mahbubul Haq, The Strategy of Economic Development: A Case Study of Pakistan (Karachi: Oxford University Press, 1963), pp. 139-40.

17. Government of Burma, The Economic Survey of Burma (1960) (Rangoon: Government Printing and Stationery Office, 1960), p. 11.

18. See Haq, op. cit., p. 137.

19. Ibid., p. 141.

20. See Hla Myint, "Economic Theory and Development Policy," Economica, XXXIV (May, 1967), 485-86.

21. Ibid., p. 486.

22. United Nations, Statistical Yearbook 1966 (New York: U.N., 1967), pp. 575-76.

23. Ibid.

24. Ibid.

25. The GDP of 1938-39 was given as K.4.945 billion; see Economic Survey of Burma, 1963 (Rangoon: Government Printing and Stationery Office, 1963), p. 5.

26. See Haq, op. cit., pp. 154-58.

27. The National Income of Burma (Rangoon: Ministry of National Planning, 1957), p. 15.

28. See, for details, R. L. Allen, "The Burmese Clearing Account Agreements," Pacific Affairs, XXXI, 2 (June, 1958).

29. Walinsky, op. cit., p. 165.

30. International Monetary Fund, International Financial Statistics (Washington, D.C.: IMF, 1961), pp. 66-67.

31. Ibid., pp. 206-7.

32. Papanek, op. cit., p. 15.

33. Ibid., pp. 17-18.

34. Outline of the 3rd Five-Year Plan. (1965-70), (Islamabad: Planning Commission, August, 1964), p. 8.

35. Walinsky, op. cit., p. 163.

36. Cf. E. E. Hagen, ed., Planning Economic Development (Homewood, Ill.: R.D. Irwin, Inc., 1963), p. 24.

37. Cf. C. Wilcox, "Pakistan," ibid., p. 64.

38. E. S. Mason, Economic Development in India and Pakistan (Cambridge: Harvard University Center for International Affairs, 1966), p. 3.

39. Premier U Nu on the Four-Year Plan (Rangoon: Directorate of Information, June, 1957), pp. 24-29.

40. Papanek, op. cit., chap. 1.

41. Report to the People by The Union of Burma Revolutionary Council on the Revolutionary Council Government's Budget Estimates for 1969-70 (Rangoon: Revolutionary Council 1969), pp. 16-17. (Hereafter cited as Report to the People....

42. U.N. Statistical Yearbook, 1966, p. 158; Papanek, op. cit., p. 7.

43. "Newsletter on Party's Affairs, No. 2, Union's Day Special" (In Burmese) (Rangoon: The Central Party Organization Committee, Burma Socialist Program Party, 1966), p. 16; also, Report to the People....

44. Papanek, op. cit., p. 7.

45. U.N., Statistical Yearbook, 1966, p. 138.

46. See International Monetary Fund, International Financial Statistics, October, 1968 (Washington, D.C.: IMF, 1968),
pp. 64-65.

47. The Working People's Daily (Rangoon: March 20, 1969),
p. 1.

48. The Philosophy of the Burma Socialist Programme
Party: The System of Correlation of Man and His Environment (Rangoon: Ministry of Information, 1963), p. 45.

49. Cf. Joseph Silverstein, "Ne Win's Revolution Reconsidered," Asian Survey, VI, 2 (February, 1966), p. 97.

50. Outline of the 3rd Five-Year Plan..., p. 8; also, Haq,
op. cit., p. 174.

51. Ibid., pp. 195-96; also, A. Moquit, A Study of Economic
Development in Pakistan (Lahore: The National Institute of
Public Administration, 1966), p. 19.

52. Outline of the 3rd Five-Year Plan..., p. 31.

53. M. Shoaid, Pakistan's Economic Growth Since 1958
(Karachi: Department of Films and Publication, 1963), p. 25.

54. Haq, op. cit., p. 175.

55. Cf. Mason, op. cit., p. 28. As he observed, "...to
the extent PL 480 imports replace commercial imports, foreign
exchange is saved."

56. Outline of the 3rd Five-Year Plan..., p. 17.

57. Ibid, pp. 35-36.

58. See, S. Rehman, "The Third Plan--An Analysis of
Objectives," A. I. Qureshi, ed., The 3rd Five-Year Plan and
Other Papers (Lahore: The Pakistan Economic Association,
1965).

59. Ministry of Finance, Pakistan Economic Indicators
(Islamabad: Ministry of Finance, 1968), p. 1.

CHAPTER **3** SOCIAL CONFLICT AND
THE IDEOLOGIES OF
DEVELOPMENT

No analysis of the origins of development goals and policies in a LDC can be complete without a scrutiny of its past
heritage. For more than a century, Pakistan and Burma had
a common colonial heritage of British rule under which social
conflicts and changes took place. The colonial impact on the
two societies has had pervasive effects, with differing intensities, on the attitudes and outlook of the political leadership that has emerged since independence. The major contrast within these changes is reflected in the development
policies and the models of economic systems adopted by the
two countries. Of the two, the colonial impact on Burma
seems to have been more traumatic. In this chapter, I will
attempt to explain how development policies in Pakistan and
Burma reflect the historical social conflict between what is
modern and what is traditional, what is alien and what is indigenous.

A CONTRAST IN COLONIAL IMPACT

Since Pakistan came into being only after the liquidation
of colonial rule, the colonial impact on Pakistan can only be
analyzed in terms of colonial policies and practices in British
India and their effect on Muslim India. Social conflict and
change were different in British India and Burma with respect
to the very process of colonization. (Burma was administered
as a province of British India until 1937.) The colonization
of Burma was accomplished through a massive importation of
foreign Orientals (Indians and Chinese), while British India
experienced no such secondary wave of alien intrusion to produce what Furnivall termed "a truly plural society."[1]
Apart from the fact that British India may be culturally
divided into Hindu and Muslim segments, there was no double

wave of alien settlement with the resulting usurpation of social
and economic opportunities by secondary alien groups. The
Hindu and Muslim Indians of the Indian subcontinent had inter-
mingled with some common interest in precolonial India. In
spite of the rigorous caste system of traditional India, the
social contact, communication and conversion between Hindus
and Muslims took place long before British colonization. This
does not mean, however, that cultural tension and social conflict did not exist between the two social groups. It simply
means that the social conflict that took place in British India
was less intense with regard to what was alien and what was
native than in Burma.

Social conflict and social change in British India took
place primarily among three basic groups--the British (including Anglo-Indians), the Muslims and the Hindus. (This
last group includes the Sikhs. Although the Sikhs are to be
regarded as a distinct subcultural group with respect to their
political and ethnic background, they are, culturally, more
akin to Hindus than to Muslims. [2] Taking Muslim India as the
pivot, the nature and time span of this social conflict may be
divided into two phases. The first phase covered a period of
protest against colonial intrusion and of general sociopolitical
unrest, during which Muslim India was eventually subordinated
to Hindu India. The British colonial policy and practice of
mistrust and disfavor toward Muslim India during that phase
arose out of the international conflict between Britain and
Russia on the issue of the status and nature of the Ottoman
Empire. The presence of Russia in Asia and its potential
threat to the Indian subcontinent led the British, at first, to
adopt a pro-Turkish policy, which was later reversed.

The reversal of this policy came about as a result of
changes in political power in England and the Great Revolt of
India in 1857. Events in Turkey, in conjunction with the so-
called Bulgarian Horror and the Mutiny of India, crystallized
the ancient Christian-Islamic conflict, which found its counterpart in British India in the form of anti-Muslim policy. The
Mutiny was attributed to the work of hostile Muslims, and the
feeling of mistrust on the part of the colonial power lingered
on into the next century. [3] From 1858 until the turn of the
century, therefore, social tension and conflict in British India
was more or less concentrated between the British and the
Muslims. The sociopolitical and economic displacement of
the Muslims by Hindus took place during that phase.

The second phase of social conflict in British India was
marked by a more congenial colonial attitude toward Muslim

India and by overt confrontation between Hindus and Muslims.
The rising tide of Indian nationalism under the leadership of
the Indian Congress and the emergence of a strong Hindu middle class had a dual effect: it created the Muslim nationalist
movement against the political and economic dominance of
the Hindus, on the one hand, and a change in British attitude
from the image of the "barbarous and untrustworthy Muslaman"
to that of the "loyal Muslaman, " on the other.[4]

The Hindu-Muslim riots in the early 1900s and the social
and political upheavals connected with the partition of Bengal
were manifestations of the impact of colonial rule and the
changes in the social system of British India, which have
continued to exert influence on the Indo-Pakistani conflict in
recent years. As early as 1875, the Hindu-Muslim social
conflict was already quite apparent under colonialism. The
view of Sayyid Ahmad Khan, which professed a procolonial
or a pro-Western attitude to regain political and intellectual
power of Muslim India from the Hindus may be taken as a case
in point.[5] The later Khilafat movement and agitation, for
example, were derived more from anti-Hindu feelings on the
part of the Muslims than from anticolonial feelings as such.
British public opinion also gave support and sympathy to the
cause of Muslim Indians. It was during the second phase,
therefore, that the roots of present Pakistani official attitudes
toward the West were planted. Contact with, and acculturation
to, the West by the Muslim elites also took place and provided
a modernized political elite in the formation of Pakistan.

As suggested, the social and political impact of colonial
rule on Muslim India was not as traumatic nor so drastic as
in Burma. By incorporating traditional Moghul systems of
administration and Islamic laws into the colonial administrative system and preserving princes and their states in British
India, the Muslim community achieved a certain historical
continuity of political leadership.[6] The same cannot be said
of colonial Burma, except for the preservation of local lords
in the Hill States--the sawbwas in the Shan State, for example.
The colonizers in Burma replaced almost all customary rules
and practices of the Burmese kingdoms, including Burmese
rulers and administrators. Based upon the Bengal model,
colonial administration in Burma was a combination of
Western-Moghul laws and practices, which relegated the
dhamathat ("Buddhist laws") and yazathat ("King's laws") to
the rural communal level.[7] (Indeed, it is a sore point among
Burmese nationalists that the civil service of Burma was
called the Indian Civil Service until after independence.)

Direct cultural contact of the Burmese with Westerners
was minimal, since the entire colonial administration of
Burma was run with trained Indian personnel. The Burmese
nationalist movements in the 1920s and the 1930s, like those
of the Muslim nationalist, were derived from anti-Indian
sentiment. As late as 1937, the dominance of the Indians
over the administrative machinery of Burma was complete,
thereby leaving very little room for the emergence of a
modernized political elite with any administrative capacity.

While traditional Burmese rulers and the army were
totally replaced, the Indian army of British India offered both
Hindus and Muslims some opportunity for military training
and for mobility within the ranks. By contrast, the Burmese
army, under the name of the Burma Rifle, was pretty much
dominated by the Indians and by minority ethnic groups, such
as the Chin and the Kachin Rifles. The real nationalist army--
the Burma Independence Army, under the command of the
Burmese--came into being only at the outbreak of World War
II.

The Burmese military elite was never trained in the West.
The famous "Thirty Heroes" (Yebaw Thongyate) were trained
in Japan to oust the British. This is not to suggest that
British colonial policy and the practice of divisive rule did not
prevail in British India. Rather, the status of the Muslims
was quite similar to that of certain ethnic minorities in
colonial Burma, whose antipathy toward the majority took the
form of loyalty and congeniality in the absorption of Western
cultural patterns.

The same colonial rule has been more traumatic for
Burma than for Pakistan or Muslim India, due to two major
differences in the nature of colonization. First, social conflict was greater in Burma in terms of both quantity and quality.
The massive invasion of secondary alien groups produced a
greater intensity of cultural antipathy and indignation on the
part of the natives. Second, the insulation of the traditional
Burmese social system, in terms of acculturation to the West,
was almost complete under the impact of colonial rule and of
the politicoreligious organizations, which dominated colonial
Burma.

Burma, unlike British India, was what E. E. Hagen has
appropriately termed "doubly colonial";[8] for Burma had to
confront a double wave of alien intrusion--the British and the
foreign Orientals. While the British annihilated the traditional polity of Burma, the Indians and Chinese dominated
the economic system, with the net effect of creating a dual

economy. Since colonization of Burma relied heavily upon
alien sources of labor and capital, its acculturation to capitalism was severely inhibited. It is not surprising, therefore,
that socioeconomic-status withdrawal and cultural antagonism
toward modernization were greater in colonial Burma than in
British India.

Although the Muslims of British India were exposed to a
similar experience in the areas of finance and commerce,
they did not have to confront the same kinds of competition
and displacement of jobs as the Burmese. J. S. Furnivall
correctly observed:

> In administration, commerce and industry, it was
> less trouble and usually cheaper to recruit Indians
> than to train Burmese; and Indians, once they
> gained a footing, naturally tended to build up an
> almost insurmountable barrier against the admission
> of Burmans. [9]

(The above statement is not only true of Indians but also of
Europeans and Chinese.)*

Domination of the small modern sector of Burma's
colonial dual economy by alien groups was evident as late as
the 1940s, when 40 percent of the urban population was still
aliens. In the 1930s, this figure was much higher; about 72
percent of the population of large towns, like Rangoon and
Moulmein, were aliens, of whom Indians made up some 50
percent. [10] The kind of social conflict and resentment resulting
from this imbalance is at the root of Burma's ideological
aversion to capitalism and continues to this day.

The severest form of alien domination occurred in the
field of financial activities, on which the entire agricultural
economy of colonial Burma depended for its functioning and
growth. There were two distinct groups of foreign Orientals
in this field, the Indian moneylenders (Chettyars), who began
their financial activities as early as 1880, and the Chinese
pawnshop owners. The former's control of the financing of
agriculture in the rural economy was irrevocably complete
by 1930, when the native cultivators were caught in a storm
of depression and indebtedness.

---

*Note that the term Burmans is used to denote the entire
native population of Burma. For the purpose of this study,
I choose to use the term Burmese to refer to the majority
ethnic group as well as the entire native population.

The Chettyars' control over cultivated land reached its
peak in 1939, when, in the thirteen principal rice-growing
districts of Lower Burma, they owned about one-half of the
land in the hands of the nonagriculturalists. (The term "non-
agriculturalist" refers to a noncultivating landowner, resident
or nonresident. During 1930-40, Chettyars' ownership grew
by four times.) The agrarian crisis of colonial Burma reflected
three major economic conditions of the cultivators' indebtedness: the tenure system, with its exorbitant rents and rates
of interest, and the alienation of cultivated land (the general
transfer of landownership to the resident and nonresident
nonagriculturalists). The estimated volume of indebtedness
was between Rs. 500 million and Rs. 600 million (an average
of £42 million). [11] It was also estimated that about 60 percent
of the cultivators were in debt and on the verge of losing their
lands. [12] A study of three major districts revealed that the
average per capita permanent indebtedness was Rs. 341, a
figure double the per capita income of Burma in 1951 (K. 172). *

In order not to exaggerate the importance of alien domination of colonial Burma's economic system, it must also be
noted that Muslim India confronted a similar situation in Hindu
domination of the financial system and the ownership of land
by Chettyars and Zamindars ("landed aristocracy"). Yet this
domination was not as complete as it was in Burma, due to
the later reversal of colonial policy, on the one hand, and the
emergence of a Muslim middle class in the latter phase of
colonial rule, on the other. It has been stated that, under the
impact of colonial rule, social disorganization in Burma was
so great that it destroyed the stability of entire communities.
E. E. Hagen, for one, has observed that successive steps
taken by the British toward the institutionalization of a modern
administrative machinery of government "had the unintended
effect of destroying the political and social basis of Burmese
community. "[13] A British administrator, B. O. Binns, affirmed this:

> The effect of the British occupation was to change
> all this [customary community and stable social
> system of Burma], to substitute a rigid centralized
> administration based on law and order for the
> elastic system of government by personalities, and

---

*Before 1952, one rupee equaled one kyat; see United
Nations, Year Book of International Trade Statistics (New
York: U.N., 1960), p. 111.

to let loose on the customary economy of the people
all the forces of that unrestrained individualism
which was a feature of 19th century economics. [14]

As suggested, social conflict in colonial Burma was so
intense that adaptation to modern ways of life came to mean
both a cultural betrayal and political serfdom to the Burmese
in general. For one thing, status usurpation and the resulting
withdrawal of traditional social and political elites were far
greater in Burma than in British India. Also, cultural homogeneity in the form of a unified value system (Buddhism) and
a politically powerful clerical order created a tension-management system. Apart from these factors, the basic economic
security of the mass of people, combined with the ascetic
value-orientation of Buddhism--in contrast to the abject
poverty and worldly traditions of those in British India--con-
tributed to the social indifference and cultural indignation of
the Burmese toward modernity. Like any other peasant
society of the world, Burmese cultivators tended to withdraw
inward in the face of any alien threat to the social security
and cultural integrity of their families and to a self-sufficient
village economy--a withdrawal made possible both by the basic
affluence of the rural economy and by the social solidarity
provided by religion.

These conditions did not prevail in British India. The
traditional social and political elites were not totally displaced
to produce the kind of social disorganization and traditional
nationalism that developed in colonial Burma. In India, the
British colonizers not only relied primarily on native sources
of labor--both skilled and unskilled, Hindu and Muslim, capital
and middlemen--but also kept certain traditional social and
political structures intact. Though it is true that Hindu administrators, financiers and merchants came to dominate the
modern sector, thereby producing strong resentment among
Muslim Indians, the traditional Muslim elites continued to
exert power and influence over Muslim communities. For the
preservation of local autonomy in the princely states and
various organizations, under hundreds of Maharajas and
Muslim rulers, had rendered a competitive political structure
of tension-management between the Hindus and Muslims, not
between the aliens and the natives or the West and the East as
such. Despite the fact that the civil service in British India
was pretty much dominated by the British, Anglo-Indians and
Hindus, the landed aristocracy and traditional political elite
of the Muslim community were allowed to exist under the dual

administration of states and provinces. By maintaining the
military tradition of Muslim rulers and continuing to use local
assemblies known as jirgas, aliens did not usurp as much
sociopolitical power in the Indian subcontinent as they did in
Burma. Acculturation of the Muslim elites, as well as marginal cultural brokers, to modernity was relatively easy in
British India by virtue of the internal Hindu threat rather than
the threat of Westerners as such. It has been observed, for
instance, that the new leaders of Muslim communities in West
Pakistan during the late nineteenth and early twentieth centuries were the old nobility and traditional landowners, on
the basis of loyal service given to the British under the system
of jagirs ("landholdings" or "revenues"). In provinces like
Bengal, where Hindus were preponderant, the new leaders did
not come from the ancient nobility but from the middle class,
which had emerged through the British educational system. [15]

The three-pronged confrontation of the Western, Hindu
and Muslim cultural systems in British India inhibited the acculturation of the Muslims to modernity less than the Buddhist
Burmese. One of the main reasons for this was that the intensive social conflict between the Hindus and Muslims, whose
fear of Hinduization outweighed their aversion to Western intrusion, produced a congeniality to Western value systems and
cultural patterns on the part of Muslim elites--particularly,
the military elite. (This congeniality has continued in the
postcolonial period.) The Muslim Indians, as the minority
social group in British India, sought social and economic
mobility through Western education and a kind of loyalty to
British rule, which was clearly revealed by the Muslim League
in its support of the British during the inter-War period and
World War II.

In colonial Burma, to a lesser degree, the same process
of acculturation and loyalty to Western rule can be discerned
in such minority social groups as the Karens, Shans and
others. These groups, in conflict with the majority Burmese,
or Bamahs, * tended to be less negative about Western value
systems and administration, a fact that was reflected in the

*The term Bamahs signifies the majority Burmese popu-
lation. A number of authors, among them J. S. Furnivall,
made use of the term Burmans to denote the entire native
population of Burma in distinguishing it from the majority
ethnic group of Burmese, or Bamahs. As stated before, I
shall use the term Burmese for all indigenous peoples of
Burma, unless otherwise specified.

religious conversion of a large segment of Karens during the
colonial period. The Christianized Karens, known as the
Sahphyu Kayin ("White Letters"), and other hill tribes, like
the Chins and Kachins, had been indignant since historical
times about majority Burmese rule. This made it easier for
them to accept Western value systems and ways of life. (In
addition, one should note that the Muslim rulers were themselves descended from aliens--from the Turks, Afghans and
Moghuls; being alien to the Indian subcontinent and different
in religion from the Hindu princes, the Muslim political elite
thus found it less necessary to reject the Western system than
the Hindu system.)

SOCIAL CONFLICT DURING AND AFTER
WORLD WAR II

     The roots of today's social and economic policies of de-
velopment in Pakistan and Burma have been immediately determined by the structure of their social systems and by the social
conflicts and changes that took place during and after World
War II. The impact of the War and the Japanese occupation
of Burma was particularly important in producing a tide of
traditional nationalism and anti-Western sentiment and creating, for the first time, a nationalist Burmese army. Political
leadership and aspirations came to be centered on the tradition
bound politicians, or Thakins, and the military elite, or Boes.
Bringing temporary unity to various factions of the Thakins,
the war years saw a corresponding decline among Western-
trained civil servants. The social conflict between the
Western-trained elite and the Thakins was not serious until
the gaining of independence, since the former took refuge in
India and elsewhere with the coming of the War.
     The Japanese occupation of Burma also created two im-
portant social changes: (a) a larger role for the tradition-
bound Burmese in the functioning of the polity and (b) the
opening of the traditional to the modern sector, through such
channels as politics and military service. The social and
economic mobility created by the War and Japanese occupation

---

     *The term "Bo" means, traditionally, the military officer
In modern times, it is interesting to note that this term has
also been used colloquially to mean a Westerner or a domin-
ating person.

was, therefore, highly significant in reviving the two most important traditional heritages, political autonomy and military power, which were embodied in the Thakins and the Boes. The interchange of political roles between the Western-trained elite and the Thakins in the administrative machinery of the Japanese interregnum widened the social and political horizons of nationalist leaders and invoked nationwide sentiment toward a return to the glorious past. Many popular songs about the glory of the head of the state, Ba Maw as Adipadi, and the courage of the "Thirty Heroes," Yebaw Thongyate, who took refuge in Japan to save Burma from the British rule, were sung throughout Burma.

While the War created social and economic mobility of tradition-bound Burmese from all social levels, the Japanese occupation made the outburst of traditional nationalism possible and reinforced the basic mistrust of aliens in general. The taste of sovereignty and independence under the puppet government of the Japanese was the Thakins' first experience with real political power after a long period of colonial subjugation.   From ministerial posts (wungyis) to the command of the Burma Independence Army, the Thakins and the Boes came to dominate the Burmese polity.   During the liquidation of colonial rule and the early years of independence, social and political conflict was evident not only between tradition-bound nationalists and the former Western-trained politicians of the colonial era but also between leftist and rightist groups among the Thakins. The assassination of General Aung San by U Saw, a former minister of the colonial government, and his followers temporarily ended the role of the military elite, and the rise of a traditionalist elite was reflected in the personality and leadership of U Nu. Despite inner social and political conflict among these groups, the inevitable impact of Japanese occupation, along with the experience of an unfulfilled self-government, has been the intensification of mistrust of alien rule. This is reflected in such Burmese sayings as "to yearn for an aunt instead of one's own mother," and: "Relying on a nat ["spirit"] from fear of a tiger turns out to be that the former is worse than the latter." In his speech at the Shwedagon Pagoda AFPFL Conference in 1946, General Aung San bluntly asserted that reliance on alien support could only make Burma a prostitute nation. This feeling of mistrust continues to prevail, with differing degrees of violence in the attitudes of civilian and military leaders of each government of the Union of Burma. The basis of neutralism, economic nationalism and socialism of successive governments lies, therefore, in political nationalism, born out of the traumatic experiences of the two consecutive foreign rules, British and Japanese.

The social and economic structure of Burma and Pakistan after their independence differed significantly, for Burma had to confront the problem of an alien-dominated dual economy. Despite massive withdrawal of alien capital by the Chettyars and the British, the presence of a large body of foreign Orientals in various fields of commerce, industry and administration was both a constant source of social conflict and a reminder of the evils of the past colonial heritage. The Land Nationalization Act and programs of Burmanization, directly aimed at getting rid of alien dominance, did not meet with much success, due to the inadequate supply of indigenous human resources and the inefficiency in implementing various governmental programs. As the tradition-bound political elite took hold of political power and moved up the social ladder, the presence not only of foreign Orientals but also of the Western-trained elite became a source of increasing indignation and ambivalence.

Thus, the underlying cause of direct governmental controls and policies of protectionism has been the inadequacy and frustration of those who gained new status and roles within the social system of Burma in governing and building a modern nation. In all processes of social conflict, the Burmese nationalist political leadership persistently uses the colonial heritage of a dual economy as the cause of developmental failures and the justification of a closed socioeconomic system. And because of its recently gained social, political and economic status, the military elite of Burma, today, is even more violent in its attitude toward other social and economic groups. Dominance of the social system of independent Burma by the Thakins, under the government of U Nu, might have been complete under the forces of traditional nationalism. Yet, under the same government, social and economic mobility via military service encouraged the rise of militant nationalism and anti-Western sentiment among military leaders. The Burmese Way to Socialism, adopted by the present Revolutionary Council Government of Burma, therefore, also reflects the social conflict and changes that took place during the independent period.

By contrast, Pakistan was formed after a bitter struggle against India abruptly ended the dominance of the Hindus. Also, the social and political structure of Pakistan was such that it did not have to confront the problem of an alien-dominated dual economy. The massive flight of Hindu financiers, land-lords and merchants, plus the exodus of Muslims from India, made up the outflow and inflow of human resources into Pakistan. Though the vacuum of the entrepreneurial function created by this flight of Hindus was never completely filled by any native reservoir of human resources, the problem of com-petition for commerce and industry between Hindus and Muslims was no longer important after partition. Moreover, jobless refugees served as a major source of labor supply for all types of occupations.

Apart from these consequences of partition, there seems to be some historical continuity of colonial institutions and social relationships in Pakistan. Dominance by Western-trained civil servants, the middle class and the military elite over the social system of Pakistan is a case in point. The Pakistani Governments' tolerance of capitalist institutions, particularly under the government of President Ayub Khan, was a direct result of pervasive effects resulting from the colonial impact and partition, on the one hand, and the basic structure of the traditional Muslim community, on the other. The rigid structure of the Muslim social system, contrasted with the more egalitarian social structure of Burma, has greatly delayed the emergence of a tradition-bound political elite from the lower social strata, which might lead to the type of social conflict that has prevailed in independent Burma. This is by no means to infer that the intensity of such a social conflict between the modernized and tradition-bound political elites is less in Pakistan than in Burma; it is rather that the dimension of the social conflict has, so far, been limited in Pakistan by the persistence of dominant political elites from the colonial past.

IDEOLOGIES OF DEVELOPMENT

Despite similar efforts to build a welfare state, and despite massive state interference with the market mechanism prior to the military interregnums, there are striking differ-ences between Pakistan and Burma in the realm of philosophy, ideology and goals of development. The most paradoxical and interesting contrast in development policies between Pakistan and Burma has been one of productivity versus equity, which does not correspond to the actual socioeconomic structure and value systems of the two societies. Despite the rigidity

of the social institutions and class barriers that exist in
Pakistan and the basic philosophy of a social collectivity or
community fostered under the Islamic religion, the attractive-
ness of modern capitalism to the Pakistani political elite has
been a paradox. Similarly, the absence of a landed aristocrac
and rigid class barriers, along with the basic Buddhist philosophy of individualism, have not engendered a congenial attitude
toward capitalism at all in independent Burma. Pakistan's
emphasis on productivity and Burma's obsession with equity
bring their own unique problems in development. These problems must be assessed in the light of social justice, on the
one hand, and the process of economic development, on the
other. For now, it is sufficient to mention that both extremes
too much emphasis on productivity and too much concern with
equity--are a direct function of social conflict in the historical
plane, and either can be disastrous to modernization. [16]

Although both nations went through a period of political
crisis and power struggle immediately after their independenc
the ideological crisis seems to have lasted longer in Pakistan.
Up until 1958, the Pakistani political scene was beset by such
colossal problems as the collapse of constitutional government
in 1954, the social dislocation and refugee problems after
partition, drawing up of the constitution, the role of Islam in
the polity and a stalemate in political party-building. [17] Even
up to the end of the Second Five-Year Plan in 1960, the proces
of development planning was said to have proceeded without a
definite "ism." [18]

In Burma, on the other hand, both the political process
and development planning have proceeded with a predilection
toward socialism from the very beginning of independence;
for the Burmese political leadership has been steadfast in
building a socialist economy, with little or no room for capitalist institutions. As early as 1945, the Naythuyein Declaration demanded explicitly that Burma follow socialism, and a
blueprint of a planned socialist economy was laid down at the
Sorrento Villa Conference of 1947 in Rangoon under the leader
ship of the late General Aung San. In 1948, three important
pieces of legislation--the Constitution, the Land Nationalizati
Act and the Two-Year Development Plan--were enacted by the
AFPFL Government of U Nu in an unshakable spirit of anticapitalism and democratic socialism.

In these documents--the Pyidawtha Conference Resolutior
and Speeches (1951) and the latest proclamation of the Burmes
Way to Socialism (1962)--the persistent theme remained an
abuse of the past colonial heritage and of capitalism. Genera

socialism in Burma has been explained on the basis of two
fundamental postulates: (a) the compatibility of socialism, or
the incompatibility of capitalism, with the traditional Buddhist
value systems and Burmese ways of life and (b) the equity and
efficiency of a socialist economic system in solving the problem of economic underdevelopment. In all fairness, it must
be noticed that both of these postulates were embraced by the
Pyidawtha Government of U Nu--not in the light of the Marxian
theses, as the Burmese Way to Socialism seems to have done,
but rather in terms of nationalism and traditionalism. [19] As
D. E. Smith put it:

> Socialist ideologies could come and go, but they
> would be judged by their relationship to a Buddhism
> which indissolubly merged with Burmese national-
> ism. Buddhism was a philosophy, but it was far
> more; it symbolized and embodied the culture and
> traditions of a renascent Burmese nation. [20]

Ideological Crisis: Process of Reconciliation
Between Modernity and Tradition

Relating Buddhist Values to Socialism

In a sense, the formal implementation of a socialist
ideology by the Burmese polity--be it the democratic socialism
of the Pyidawtha Government or the Marxist socialism of the
present Revolutionary Council Government--actually represented an ideological crisis, rather than an accomplishment,
in the process of reconciliation between modernity and tradition. Inasmuch as the failures of the U Nu Government
stemmed from the inadequacy of relating Buddhist values to
those of modern socialism, so the recent failures of the
Revolutionary Council Government arise from the inability of
the military elite to disseminate the Marxist-oriented Burmese
Way to Socialism in terms of traditional Buddhist philosophy
and value systems.

The clearest examples of this crisis can be found in the
speeches of both U Nu and his socialist colleagues of the
AFPFL Party and in the latest philosophy of the BSPP, as
propounded in the official text, The System of Correlation of
Man to His Environment. While U Nu defined his ideal socialist
society as the one that "would promote economic equality,
discourage the acquisitive instinct in man, and provide

sufficient leisure so that virtually everyone in the entire society
could devote time to meditation for nibbana,"[21] the Burmese
Way to Socialism defined the ideal economic system as one
that avoids "vulgar materialism" and annihilates "the pernicious
economic system in which man exploits man, and self-interest
and self-seeking are the motivating forces."[22]

Even though the Burmese Way to Socialism and its concept of an ideal socialist society seems to have fewer religious
overtones, the substantive reasons for embracing the Marxian
theses are given in Buddhistic metaphysical concepts, such
as the three worlds (lokas), impermanency (annica) and greed
(loba).[23] From the standpoint of conflict between modernity
and traditionalism, therefore, the ideological identity of the
Burmese political leadership with the modern tenets of
socialism is, actually, a delusion. Behind the political facade
of the Burmese Way to Socialism lies the deep-seated problem
of attempting to create a modern nirvana within traditional
images of a Pyidawtha--a classless society of opulence, peace
and happiness without greed, desire and anger. (Greed (loba),
desire (mawha) and anger (dawtha) are the three modes of
nescience responsible for suffering in Buddhism.)[24] In view
of the egalitarian social structure of Burma, the Marxist
dialectical process of class struggle and historical materialism
which are abundantly employed by the theorists of the Burmese
Way to Socialism in their reinterpretation of Burmese history,
is a myth. The Hegelian dialectical process of conflicts and
contradictions, on the other hand, is more applicable to the
search for an ideological identity in independent Burma, where
the force of traditionalism has plunged the nationalist political
leadership into a prolonged crisis of social inertia in the pragmatic realm of effective action for development. It is in this
sense of incessant preoccupation with the idealistic philosophy
of "traditionalized socialism" that the political leadership of
Burma has failed disastrously, as compared with Pakistan,
in development planning.

Relating Islamic Values to Welfare State

In the first decade of independence, the Pakistani ideological crisis was quite similar to Burma's, as far as relating
the traditional Islamic value systems and ways of life to those
of a welfare state are concerned, though the Pakistani political
leadership was less indignant about its colonial heritage and
about capitalism. Theoretical polemics on the role and function of Islam in the Pakistani polity took place in much the

same manner as did the debates on Marxism versus Buddhism
that occurred among Burmese politicians. The difference in
their search for ideological identity was that Pakistan came
into being as an independent nation without any specific predilection to socialism or traditionalism as such. The rigorous
proposals of the Islamization of the Pakistani polity by tradition-
bound political groups, such as the Jammatt-i-Islami, for instance, were rejected and defeated quite early in Pakistan by
the modernists and, particularly, by the Westernized political
and military elites. [25]
    The secularization of the polity was easier in Pakistan
than in Burma, due to the fact that the social and political
structures of Islam do not separate the state from the church;
the legitimacy of the power of the head of a Muslim State does
not need the sanctioning of the clerical order, since he is considered to be the spiritual as well as the temporal leader of
the society. This traditional heritage, dating back to the system of Caliphate in ancient Arabia, made it easier for alienated
political elites in Pakistan to cope with the problems of social
and religious protest inherent in the process of modernization.
As L. Binder put it, "The Islamic theology can give no sanction
at all to whatever system of constitutional law may be de-
vised"[26] by the political rulers. Moreover, Pakistan was
brought into existence by the efforts of the Westernized middle
class of British India--the landed aristocracy, the civil servants,
and the military officers--upon whom the task of government
of the new Muslim state fell completely. [27] The struggle for
a Muslim state by the ulamas, the learned men of the Islamic
Law (Shariat), was said to have been quite ambiguous and
ambivalent, [28] although they registered a strong protest against
the secularization of the Pakistani polity in the early years of
independence. Orthodox traditionalist groups, such as the
ulamas, the Jammatt-i-Islami and the Nizam-i-Islami, along
with the students and the Muslim community (umma), demanded
the Islamization of the polity and the revival of traditionalism,
without much success, against the overpowering modernists
and secularists, represented by the politicians, civil servants
and military elite. [29]
    The excursion of the traditionalists (ulamas) and funda-
mentalists (Jammatt-i-Islami) into the Pakistani political
process was abortive, not because the invocation of religion
and traditions was ineffective in the creation of a Muslim state
but because both the social structure of Islam and of British
India had engendered some institutional bases for modernization and secularization. While the religiosity of political

leaders as a source of legitimacy and social sanctioning of
political power might be considered as important in Pakistan
as in Burma, the absence of ecclesiastical structure in the
social structure of Islam is an asset in the development of a
secular state. Although one may concur with the view that the
crucial weakness of Islam lies in its inability to provide nation
leadership, [30] this very weakness may be viewed as a factor
conducive to the process of secularization of the Pakistani
polity. In spite of the traditional theory of the pious sultan,
the intellectual compartmentalization of religious and adminis
trative functions of the Muslim rulers since the days of the
Caliphate has given the Pakistani political elites the freedom
of secular power from the encroachment of religious functionaries, such as the ulamas and pirs. [31] This was quite
evident in the firm stands taken by the first premier, Liaquat
Ali Khan, against the demands of orthodox traditionalists at
the very dawn of independence[32]--demands for Islamic dis-
pensation, the Islamization of the country's polity and the
making of law by the traditional consensus (ijma) of the Muslin
community. Not to exaggerate the secularist tendencies of
the Pakistani polity, it should be remembered that the ideolog
cal crisis of the Muslim League Government of Pakistan was
quite similar to that of Burma's AFPFL Government in its
inability to reconcile traditionalism with modernity, on the
one hand, and religion with politics, on the other. In the
words of W. A. Wilcox, the constitutional morass of Pakistan
under civilian government was due to the fact that

> the concern with Islam, begun in an effort to awaken
> a particular people to their earthly plight and not
> their theology, became an obsession, a neo-
> orthodox and final heterodox monster, the self-
> same creature the Muslim League leadership had
> hoped to slay. [33]

Development of a Modernized Elite

Although it may be inferred that both the Pakistani and
Burmese political leadership attempted to return to the gloric
past via the revival of traditions in the name of religion, [34]
the sociopolitical structure of Pakistan was more viable than
Burma's in the development of a modernized elite. This was
largely due to Pakistan's colonial heritage of a strong middle
class and a bureaucracy--no matter how small in size--and t

the weakness of religious functionaries in nationalist political
movements. It was no accident that the administrative machinery of Pakistan's governments was dominated by Western-
oriented civil services and the entire polity by middle-class
and military elites with an affinity for Western value systems.
The British policy of religious neutrality, along with continuation of the princely states in British India, had created a
sociopolitical structure in which the traditional roles and
functions of Hindu and Muslim rulers were maintained to absorb Western values and methods. The same cannot be said
of Burma, where a similar policy of religious neutrality
stimulated the growth of political activity among Buddhist
monks, [35] or thanghas, * and a policy of replacing the traditional kingship's rule of will by the Western rule of law created
intense ambivalence toward civil servants. Also, the Burmese
middle class and its civil servants actually ran the administrative machinery autonomously only after 1937, whereas in
Pakistan or British India the dominance of the civil service
lasted more than a century. Furthermore, the Indian Civil
Service, to which a very few Western-trained Burmese be-
longed as subordinate administrators, dominated the governing of Burma as a part of British India. In their acculturation
to Western value systems and ways of life, the Burmese elites
were not only given less opportunity for absorption but also
had to confront a formidable tide of traditional indignation and
protest directed against Westernization by the politically active
sanghas.
     The entire nationalist movement of colonial Burma was,
thus, inextricably intertwined with Buddhism, and the sanghas,
who became associated with such politicoreligious organizations
as the General Council of the Buddhist Association and the
Young Men's Buddhist Association, as well as with politically
prominent monks, such as U Ottama and U Wisara. This is
not to undermine the role of the Western-oriented political
leaders--Ba Maw and Maung Maung Gyi, for instance--in the
nationalist movement, but to state that the secularist political
ideology expressed in the Marxist-oriented Thakin political
movement was de facto more traditional than modern in its
source of inspiration. From the Thakins' political slogan,
showing the Burmese to be descendants of the ancient master
or ruling race, to the image of a Pyidawtha of U Nu, the
romantic appeal to the glorious past and the cultural superiority

---

*Thanghas is a Burmese term for sanghas, Buddhist
priests in Pali.

of Buddhist value systems and philosophy over those of
Western systems had been the sine qua non of the Burmese
polity.

The recent Burmese Way to Socialism is no exception to
this historical societal bias. The anti-Western spirit, along
with an anticapitalist bias and the relentless pursuit of socialis
in independent Burma, may, thus, be seen as a historical
continuum of nationalist response to the Western colonial intrusion. In the words of J. S. Furnivall, it may be concluded:
"Because capitalism had worked to their disadvantage they
mistrusted capital. And because capital is derived from
profit, they mistrusted profit as an incentive to industry.
And they associated capitalism with foreign rule."[36] Though
this historical explanation of Burmese indignation toward
capitalism is largely correct, the simple historical reason
is insufficient for total comprehension of the paranoia and the
inward-looking character of the Burmese polity. It is also
necessary to look into value systems and cultural patterns to
account for the relative degrees of societal openness.

                                NOTES

        1. See J. S. Furnivall, Colonial Policy and Practice
(New York: New York University Press, 1956), p. 307.

        2. See O. H. K. Spate, India and Pakistan: A General
and Regional Geography (London: Methuen & Co., 1954), pp.
130-32.

        3. See, for details, K. K. Aziz, Britain and Muslim
India (London: Heineman, 1963), pp. 24-30.

        4. Ibid., p. 17.

        5. Ibid., pp. 28-30; see, also, M. Mujeeb, The Indian
Muslims (Montreal: McGill University Press, 1967), chap.
xix.

        6. See, for details, Percival Spear, India, Pakistan,
and the West (4th ed.; New York: Oxford University Press,
1967), chap. 8; also, Hugh Tinker, The Foundations of Local
Self-Government in India, Pakistan and Burma (London: The
Athlone Press, 1954), chap. ii. He seems to argue that no

indigenous source of local government was incorporated into the colonial administrative system. I contend to the contrary for the case of Pakistan.

7. See Maung Maung, Burma's Constitution (The Hague: Martinus Nighoff, 1959), Part I.

8. E. E. Hagen, "Allocation of Investment in Under-developed Countries: Observations Based Upon the Experience of Burma," Massachusetts Institute of Technology Center for International Studies, Investment Criteria and Economic Growth (Cambridge, Mass.: M.I.T. Press, 1955), p. 66.

9. Furnivall, op. cit., p. 117.

10. J. J. Bennison, Census of India, 1931, Burma (Rangoon: Government Printing and Stationery Office, 1933), XI, Part I, 44-45.

11. Report of the Burma Provincial Banking Enquiry Committee (1920-1930) (Rangoon: Government Printing and Stationery Office, 1931), I, 54.

12. Ibid., p. 55.

13. E. E. Hagen, On the Theory of Social Change (Home-wood, Ill.: The Dorsey Press, 1963), p. 462.

14. B. O. Binns, The Agricultural Economy of Burma (Rangoon: Government Printing and Stationery Office, 1948), p. 2.

15. See, for details, D. N. Wilber, Pakistan: Its People, Its Society, Its Culture (New Haven, Conn.: Human Relations Area Files Press, 1964), chap. 7; also, R. V. Weeks, Pakistan: Birth and Growth of a Muslim Nation (Princeton, N.J.: D. Van Nostrand Co., 1964), chap. 8.

16. See Max F. Millikan, Modernization, Myron Weiner, ed. (New York: Basic Books, Inc., 1966).

17. See, for details, Z. A. Suleri, Pakistan's Lost Years: Being a Survey of a Decade of Politics (1948-58) (Karachi: Progressive Papers Ltd., 1962), Introduction.

18. Mahbubul Haq, The Strategy of Economic Development
A Case Study of Pakistan (Karachi: Oxford University Press,
1963), p. 198. In fact, the author anticipated tighter social
and economic controls of the Pakistani economy after the
Second Five-Year Plan, which, of course, turned out to be
wrong.

19. See, for details, Mya Maung, "Socialism and Economi
Development of Burma, " Asian Survey, IV, 12 (December,
1964).

20. D. E. Smith, Religion and Politics in Burma (Princeton, N. J. : Princeton University Press, 1965), p. 132. He
also stated that "ideology was always a secondary concern, a
fact which enabled important theoretical shifts to take place
with a minimal of intra-party conflict. " Ibid. I concur only
partially with that conclusion, since behind the facade of unity
in religion among the political leaders, there has always been
ideological rift as to the place of Buddhism in Burmese politic

21. U Nu, "What is Socialism? " Pyidaungsu Niti, Guide fo
the Peoples of the Union of Burma, 1959 (Rangoon: Ministry
of Information, 1959), p. 10; quoted by Richard Butwell in
"The Four Failures of U Nu's Second Premiership, " Asian
Survey, Vol. II (March, 1962).

22. The Philosophy of the Burma Socialist Programme
Party: The System of Correlation of Man and His Environmen
(Rangoon: Ministry of Information, 1963), p. 44.

23. Ibid. , pp. 3-15.

24. See Bhikkhu Ananda Metteyya, The Religion of
Burma (Madras: Theosophical Publishing House, 1929), pp.
112-78.

25. Suleri, op. cit. , pp. 7-14.

26. L. Binder, Religion and Politics in Pakistan (Berkele
University of California Press, 1961), p. 22.

27. Ibid. , chap. ii.

28. Karl von Vorys, Political Development in Pakistan
(Princeton, N. J.: Princeton University Press, 1965), pp.
130-31.

29. Cf. Binder, op. cit. , pp. 7-36.

30. Karl von Vorys, op. cit. , p. 41.

31. Cf. Binder, op. cit. , pp. 12-20.

32. Suleri, op. cit. , pp. 7-14.

33. W. A. Wilcox, Pakistan: The Consolidation of a
Nation (New York: Columbia University Press, 1963), p. 166.

34. Ibid.

35. Cf. Smith, op. cit. , pp. 40-43.

36. J. S. Furnivall, The Economy of Burma (Rangoon:
1952), p. 9. (Privately published.)

CHAPTER **4** A CLOSED SOCIETY
VERSUS AN OPEN
SOCIETY

At the outset, it must be remembered that, in terms of
historical societal contact and international mobility of culture, hardly any society can be labeled "closed." Burma and
Pakistan, as products of sociocultural configuration derived
from Sino-Indian and Indo-Arabic civilizations, are no exception to this. In modern times, both societies have been sub-
jected to British colonial rule and, more recently, to the
process of bipolaric diffusion of ideologies, capital and technology by Western and Sino-Soviet blocs. With respect to the
importation or imitation of advanced models of economic
growth, therefore, Burma and Pakistan cannot be compared
as a "closed society" versus an "open society."

Where social conflict and economic change are concerned
however, a social system can be viewed as closed with respec
to the elasticity of social change, the intensity of social conflict and its policies of sociocultural insulation generated by
the forces of a traditional social system. It is in this sense
that Burma's development strategy and policies offer an interesting contrast to those of Pakistan. The social and economic policies of independent Burma have been more vitiated
by its historic antipathy toward Western intrusion; this, in
turn, reflects the backlash effect of British colonial rule and
leads to what has been described as an "inward-looking"
nation.* Pakistan's policies, on the other hand, have been

---

*The term "inward-looking" is misleading in regard to
the absorption and imitation by LDCs of the advanced methods
forms and ideologies of social and economic organization.
The process of development planning in most LDCs today is
ipso facto outward-looking, under the impact of what economists call "the demonstration effect." Cf. Hla Myint, "Economic Theory and Development," Economica, XXXIV (May,
1967), 485-86.

more "outward-looking, " or open, in regard to the absorption
of outergenerated technological and economic capital. It is
this contrast in the degree of societal openness that accounts
for the relative pace of development in Burma and Pakistan.
In this chapter, my thesis will be that not only the historical
circumstances but also the traditional sociocultural heritage
of Pakistan is more open than that of Burma.

A COMPARATIVE ANALYSIS OF CULTURES

It is, indeed, paradoxical that the same colonial influence
produced opposite responses in Pakistan and Burma regarding
sensitivity to the Western inflow of values, capital and technology. In the light of the social dynamics presented previously, a simple historical explanation alone is insufficient;
there must also be a consideration of differences in value
systems, cultural institutions, socioeconomic structures and
circumstances between the two countries. A comparative
analysis of their social systems also offers interesting paradoxes regarding the role of social institutions in the development of ideologies.

In the first place, Islamic value systems and cultural
institutions seem generally more susceptible to socialism
than their Burmese counterparts. The philosophy of Islam
tends to foster a collective social consciousness, which is
reflected in the concept of the Muslim community (millat):
the universal brotherhood and equality of believers, the social
consensus (ijma) and the unity of God (Tauhid). [1] By contrast,
the Buddhist philosophy tends to desocialize the individual and
is reflected in such concepts as karma (kan in Burmese):[2]
the inequality of the status of individuals due to the good or
bad kan, detachment as the way to nirvana, or nibban, and individual effort (wiriya) to attain station in life. But these
features of religious belief seem to have little bearing upon
the development of economic ideologies in the two countries.
The ascetism contained in both religions, however, tends to
inhibit the development of acquisitiveness or capitalism. The
Koran's prohibition on usury (riba), along with its stress on
almsgiving (zakat and sadaqat) and pilgrimage (hijji), are
similar to the Buddhist emphasis on deeds of merit (ahlu, or
"almsgiving") and meditation (dah-na); in both cases, the
philosophy seems to work against the emergence of an acquisitive society.

In terms of the social consciousness of a collectivity and
of ascetic values, Pakistan would seem to be more open to
the formation of a socialist society than Burma. Yet, neither
the traditional values and institutions of Islam nor its rigid
social structure has promoted socialism in Pakistan. The
crucial point here is that religious philosophy and value systems per se cannot be taken as a static parameter for explaining the roots of development ideologies and policies. To most
observers, for example, Burmese individualism ought to be
quite compatible with the capitalist economic system. But,
in retrospect, the influence of Buddhism is more on spiritual
and intellectual matters than on economic effort and action.
Looking at the basic tenets of Burmese Buddhism, individualis
seems to stand out in theory. In reality, there is an enormous
gap between the ideal and the real or between religious theory
and practices. The spirit of reliance on social approval for
individual actions is certainly strong in Burma, as it is in
other parts of the less developed world. A lack of corres-
pondence between the religious ideal and the reality of social
life is common to both Pakistan and Burma, and one must
look elsewhere to explain the divergent pattern of development
ideologies.
        The real patterns of culture, both economic and social,
in Pakistan and Burma also fail to provide answers to these
paradoxes. One might argue, for instance, that rigorous
stratification of the traditional, as well as the modern, social
system of Pakistan makes the rise of socialism impossible.
In terms of Marxist--as well as Schumpeterian--theses, such
a class structure might be considered a favorable condition
for takeoff into the classic class struggle and ready acceptance
of socialism. Such is not the case; Pakistan's traditional and
colonial social system has been characterized by an enormous
gap between the religious ideal of universal brotherhood or
equality and the real social structure. In ancient Arabia and
Pakistan alike, social distinctions, based upon blood, caste
and occupation, have been central to the Muslim society. [3]
In Pakistan, differentiation between the nobility (ashraf) and
the commoners (ajlaf), the landed aristocracy and the peasantr
the chieftain (choudry) and the villagers, the soldiers and the
craftsmen (kammis)[4]--all would seem to provide favorable
conditions for the development of socialism within the theory
of dialectical materialism. It can be argued, of course, that
the prominence of the bourgeoisie and their economic power
inhibit the growth of socialism. Be that as it may, if one
accepts the theses of the poverty or "immiserization" of the

masses[5] and the exploitation of the proletariat by the bourgeoisie as the stimuli for the downfall of capitalism, the
socioeconomic structure of Pakistan would seem to be more
suited to socialism than Burma's.

More intriguing is the case of Burma, where the relentless pursuit of socialism does not have as its source the
actual socioeconomic structure of either traditional or independent Burma. On the contrary, the Burmese social system
has been credited with encouraging democracy and individualism.
To most observers, both Burmese and foreign, the egalitarian
and individualistic nature of the country's social system seems,
at first, to be most impressive.[6] Compared to classic India
or Pakistan, Burma's social structure--in the absence of a
caste system--is far more conducive to social and economic
mobility. Colonial rule, also, had encouraged individualism
and destroyed some traditional social distinctions. Paradoxically, without any significant landed aristocracy or a middle
class--especially since independence--the Burmese case has
in effect shattered both the class struggle and the poverty
theses of dialectical materialism in its absorption of socialism.
Indeed, this may be the precise reason for Burma's failure
in its experiment with socialism. The appeal of socialism to
the Burmese nationalist political leadership or the appeal of
modern capitalism to the Pakistani leadership, therefore,
lies not in the static parameters of either religion or the socioeconomic structure as such, but in the historical process of
social conflict and change that took place in the traditional
social system during and after colonial rule.

Perhaps the answer lies in the area of personality formation in Burmese and Pakistani families; yet, microstructural
studies of personality fail to explain satisfactorily and consistently why certain patterns of ideology and social renovation occur in a particular traditional society.[7] The general
theory of social change, based upon neo-Freudian theses of
authoritarian versus innovational personalities (see E. E.
Hagen), reveals a puzzling exception in Pakistan. One might
think that the greater degree of authoritarianism and the most
conspicuously ascriptive Muslim culture, which can be seen
in the patriarchal and the family lineage systems of Pakistan,
would have tended to repress innovation and innovational personalities.

It has been observed that the source of the entrepreneurial
function in Pakistan is generally found in the traditional sector
rather than in the Westernized social groups--a factor that is
used to shatter the Weberian thesis of marginal cultural

brokers and E. E. Hagen's theory of status withdrawal. [8]
This argument, of course, ignores the fact that the Westernize
native social groups are not necessarily innovators in most
LDCs. They are, in fact, mostly professional groups, with
a value-orientation toward white-collar types of occupation,
the civil service and a host of other nonbusiness professions.
The main reason for the attraction of these professions was
that they carried with them symbols of the prestige, mastery
and authority of the colonial rulers. [9] Despite its limitations,
the personality formation of a child, together with the religiou
and cultural orientation of the traditional social system, is
highly important in assessing the viability of a culture for
modernization. I suspect, at least in the case of Burma, that
cultural, physical and historical conditioning of personality
tends to repress innovation more so than its Pakistani counterparts.

The simple contention that no experience of "traditional"
and stagnant societies of the Western world in the infancy of
its development has any relevancy, whatsoever, to the case
of Pakistan is too relativistic and minimizes the importance
of traditional barriers to economic change. [10] In the experience of Pakistan, the so-called appropriate and pragmatic
policies of development and the positive responses to the
stimulation of private incentives did not come about accidental-
ly. Rather, they have emerged in a complex sociopolitical
and economic setting, and their raison d'être must be sought
in the dynamics of social change rather than in the functional
emphasis of "what is, must be." [11] In other words, the source
of appropriate policies and the positive responses to them
must be explored within the traditional, as well as transitional
social systems of the particular countries under consideration.
The appeal of a particular economic system to a traditional
society stems from the ideational and emotional level of that
society in the process of social conflict and is, therefore,
profoundly influenced by its basic value system and culture.
It is also a function of the type of leadership that has come
to dominate the polity. It is my contention that the traditional
social system of Pakistan is more open than that of Burma in
terms of social conflict and cultural configuration.

A Contrast in Societal Openness

In the whole spectrum of social conflict and cultural configuration, the nationalist leadership's choice of ideologies

and policies of development is conditioned by two sets of
factors--those of internal environment and those of external
historical factors. The internal environmental factors relate
to the nature and structure of the traditional social system,
the historical ones to the forces of cultural configuration, international conflict and external environment in which Pakistan
and Burma have emerged and must function as independent
nations. The relative openness of Pakistani society to the
inflow of external technology and capital, as opposed to the
relatively closed quality of Burma, may be explained in terms
of the traditional heritage and international social conflict
during and after colonial rule. Some of these have already
been given.

In spite of the functional argument that most religions
are integrative in solidifying the social system, it is my contention that the degree of integration differs from country to
country with respect to societal rejection of outside values,
cultures and technology. Some countries managed to develop
a secularized ethic and philosophy earlier than others, either
because of a given heterogeneity of value systems, subcultures
and social conflict or because of the alienation of certain social
and political elites. In Pakistan, the intermingling of alien
and native cultures and value systems took place long before
British colonialism. The historical process of Muslim cultural configuration in India was such that it provided secular-
istic and worldly traditions for modernization.

The intermingling of both Muslims and Hindus and their
value systems in the process of religious conversion of the
Hindus from a lower strata of the Indian social system, along
with the Indo-Arabic acculturation, is the basis of its open
social system. In precolonial India, there were more than
three basic religions and hundreds of subcultural groups,
with their respective aristocracies, sects and value systems,
which, at once, created a heterogeneous cultural system of
tension, conflict and acculturation. Islam, Hinduism, Sikhism,
Buddhism and Zoroastrianism cut across the entire Indian
subcontinent in such a way that there was no single overriding
sociocultural system to close the traditional society from
outside encroachment, as Buddhism has historically done in
Burma. This variety of traditional value systems, with the
resulting religious competition among Muslims, Hindus and
Sikhs, for instance, has become the basis for reforms and
change in the religious movements of Punjab. [12]

This cultural diversity and social conflict continued
throughout the colonial era, so that the Islamic religion, from

the very beginning of its birth in India, had to contend with
rival religions as well as the internal divisions of sects and
castes in a way that Burmese Buddhism never experienced.
It is not surprising, therefore, that except for a minor split
of the Karma and Dwaya sects over the issues of the meaning
of karma, or kan, and the religious conduct of the monks in
the colonial period, Buddhism in Burma has not undergone
any significant internal transformation for the development
of a secularized ethical system. The Islamic religion, on
the other hand, has been subject to both theoretical contro-
versies and sectarianism throughout its history. Such con-
troversies as those between the Sunnis and the Shias, the
Sufists and the Purists, and the traditionalists and modernists,
as well as the entire issue of making Pakistan an Islamic
state, reflect the multiplicity of the traditional social system.

Both physically and culturally, therefore, Pakistan may
be called relatively open in the historical absorption of alien
value systems. Though the physical factors of societal openness are no longer important in modern times, the geographic
barriers to alien intrusion in the early cultural individuation
of a country may be taken as important in the process of social
conflict, change and cultural development. In India or Pakistan
physical proximity to the Middle East and the accessibility of
both aliens and indigenous populations to the outside world
may be considered as part of this societal openness. The invasion of the Turks, Afghans, Iranians and Moghuls into
Western India, for example, was far easier than the penetration of the Tatars, Chinese and Indians into Burma, a country
whose mountainous terrain enhances its physical isolation--
except for the southern seacoast. The outward-looking character of the Indians or Pakistanis is both physically and culturally inherent in their traditional social system. Physical
accessibility, coupled with a traditional cultural heritage of
wandering nomads and economic insecurity of the land, have
served both as push factors for the emigration of Indians
abroad and for the country's receptivity to alien technology
and capital. Such heritages are lacking in Burma to make
its social system more inward-looking or closed.

Of the cultural factors, societal insulation from outside
encroachment is to be found in the solidity of religion with
respect to its integrative function in a particular culture.
The Islam of Pakistan, as described above, has been less
unifying with respect to the process of cultural resistance to
the inflow of alien values and technology than has Burmese
Buddhism. This is not because the Islamic religion is more

liberal than Buddhism as such. In fact, Islam, like orthodox
Christianity, may be deemed more stringent and puritanical
with regard to the priesthood, fasting and other religious disciplines than its Buddhist counterparts. Maybe the very
liberality of Buddhism and its easier religious disciplines are
the cause of disorganizational tendencies in the Burmese personality. As far as puritanism is concerned, Islam has a
greater affinity to Christianity than Buddhism. For, in
Buddhism, there seems to be no equivalent concept of religious calling, as is found in Calvinistic ethics or the ijtehad
of Islam. [14]

It has been observed, for instance, that although the emphasis on Islam was most effective in unifying the whole movement for Pakistan by generating sociopolitical momentum
against the perils of Hinduization, the same emphasis promoted
conflict and sectarianism in Pakistan after partition; that is,
Islam was unifying in India and divisive in Pakistan. [15] The
reason for this can only be found in the multiplicity of value
systems and subcultural groups in the traditional social system
of Muslim India. The same was not true of Burma, where
Buddhism has been the single unifying force throughout its
entire history. Traditional nationalism in Burma derived its
main vigor from Buddhism, while in British India, the development of nationalism was less traditional, due to the nature of
Hinduism and Islam, which militated against it. [16] In this
perspective, the inward-looking character of Burma's development policies comes into focus as a process of social conflict
and resistance to the alien inflow of values, cultures and
technology.

Another equally important factor in the relative attraction
of capitalism or socialism to Pakistan and Burma can be found
in the basic tenets of Islam and Buddhism, together with their
respective cultural heritages. In the history of the development of Islam, one finds endless commentaries and debates,
indicating the basic elements of tension and cultural conflict.
For the actual tenets of Islam are few and not essentially different from the basic dogmas of Christianity. [17] In Pakistan
and other lands of Islam, folk elements, mysticism and cultural variation pervaded the Islamic fraternities. It has been
observed, for example, that "unorthodox practices abound in
Pakistan, particularly among illiterate Muslims who have
lived intimately among Hindus, as in Sind and East Pakistan. "[18]
The same may be said of Burmese Buddhism regarding the
folk elements that appeared in the form of the worship of spirits
(nats). [19] In Burma, however, the distinction between orthodox

and unorthodox practices of Buddhism is hardly present,
since the challenge to, and debate over, the scriptures are
virtually absent among laymen. This is not to say that
Buddhism in Burma has been static or stagnant, but to point
out that to most Buddhist Burmese the authority of the scriptures and priests (thanghahs) is absolute. Indeed, very few
commentaries and debates over the Tripitakat ("Three Baskets") appeared in the religious thought of Burma. Successive
socialist governments of the Union of Burma, in fact, have
constantly urged purification of Buddhism, without too much
success. Compared with the history of Islam in Pakistan,
therefore, the Buddhism of Burma and its reinterpretations
are rather late in time.

        Having differed substantially in the ontological and epis-
temological realm, Islam and Buddhism may be conceived of
as equally strong in their injunction against acquisitiveness.
Yet, the cultural inhibition against acquisitiveness in Pakistan
is certainly less in the light of both the teachings of the Koran
and the worldly traditions of Muslims. The Koran, for exampl
commands: "Let there be amongst you Traffic and Trade by
Mutual Good Will, " whereas the dharma dictates that the desire for, and attachment to, wealth, property and worldly
pleasure is the underlying cause of sufferings (dokka), and
the true path to nirvana lies in the overcoming of desires. *
In combination with traditional Muslim practices of a levy on
the right to acquire and maintain property, as well as the
heritage of trade, traffic and travel, and the rewarding of land
revenue (jagirs) to military servicemen, the Islamic religion
sanctions the ownership of property and conduct of business.
As R. Levy observed:

        Within the broad classes of Islamic society and
        sometimes drawing from all of them are groupings
        which have at various times and places come about
        on the basis of some common interest, that might
        be a handicraft, a sport, a religious "reform, "
        a political impulse, trading expediency or a combin-
        ation of two or more. 20

Occupational groups, or trade guilds, have existed among
Indians since long before the birth of Islam. 21 In Burma, also

_____

        *These are two of the Four Noble Truths in Buddhism;
see Ledi Sayadaw, "Manual of the Four Noble Truths, " The
Light of the Dhamma, op. cit. , VI, 1.

there were practices by the Burmese kings of land rewards
and the right to levy taxes to military servicemen and artists.
But there were no equivalent traditions of occupational groups,
trade and traffic, since the religion does not sanction acquisitiveness.

From the Koran's sanctioning of trade and a trading pro-
fession[22] to the Indo-Arabic traditions of seafaring, traveling
and city-dwelling Muslims*--along with the occupational
specialization of Hindu-Muslim castes--the traditional sociocultural system of Pakistan is far more tolerant of the quality
of acquisitiveness. [23] The ascetic emphasis of Buddhism,
plus the traditional Burmese disapproval of the merchant class
(athe, or konthe) and the middlemen (pwezas), has tended to
repress acquisitiveness for its own sake. [24] This traditional
bias by no means deters the Burmese from the enjoyment of
material welfare, [25] but it has served as a norm of conduct,
which is clearly revealed in the Burmese prejudice against
profit-making institutions. The colonial social and economic
impact further deepened this bias, through social conflict with
economically more aggressive foreign Orientals. Indians in
Burma, for example, have been labeled "stingy savers" and
"ruthless money-mongers," indicating a cultural protest
against capitalism under the impact of Buddhism.

To confirm W. A. Lewis' thesis that ascetism of traditional religions is not an economic drag on the enjoyment of
material welfare and input of effort given the right opportunities and a wider socioeconomic horizon, [26] it is certainly true
that many Burmese began to take up modern professions and
to engage in business in the later part of the colonial period.
Nevertheless, I shall argue that the value-orientation of the
Buddhist Burmese, in conjunction with their historical experiences of capitalism, has been more congenial and receptive to modern socialist ideals than to capitalist ones.

The pursuit of socialism in independent Burma not only
fits its traditional value systems, it also fits the personality
of the tradition-bound nationalist leadership and the type of
social conflict and change that took place after the liquidation
of colonial rule. Marxian moral and political overtones--the
exploitation of the masses by morally degenerate capitalists

---

*As Levy observed, one of the reasons for the greater
growth of Muslim over Hindu communities in Bengal was "the
fact being as a rule (Muslims) are town-dwellers and not
cultivators in so large a proportion as Hindus, they are less
liable to be caught by famine," op. cit., p. 42.

or bourgeoisie--are appealing to traditionally oriented
Burmese, who, equally, denounce pecuniary and worldly
motives. In line with Weber's thesis, it is true that, in spite
of certain sporadic and random modifications of the ascetic
ethics of Burmese Buddhism--revealed in the Lawka Niti
("The Worldly Laws"), or in such sayings as, "Without a full
stomach, one cannot meditate"--the secularization of Buddhist
ethics has not taken place to bring about any real social acceptance of capitalism.

Pakistani value systems, on the other hand, have undergone significant secularization and changes, which are most
clearly discernible in the works of the philosopher-poet,
Mohammad Iqbal; of his followers, such as F. K. Khan Durran
Niyaz, K. G. Sayyidayn and others;[27] and the modern philosop.
of political leaders such as Sayyid Ahmad, Mohammad Ali
Jinnah (Quaid-i-Azam), Liaquat Ali Khan and General Ayub
Khan. Iqbal, for example, wrote that to make "desire," the
ancient devil of the religious, into a prime good,

Keep desire alive in thy heart
Lest thy little dust become a tomb. [28]

He further discoursed on the role of man in the universe:
"It is the lot of man to share in the deeper aspirations of the
universe around him and to shape his own destiny as well as
that of the universe."[29] This modern interpretation of religion is in contrast to the Burmese Buddhist concepts of kan
and annica ("impermanency"), which have received very little
modernized interpretation in the work of any lay philosopher.
Although the idea of kan is originally derived from the Pali
word Kri, meaning action or work, the deterministic and
fatalistic interpretation of it is strong in Burmese belief. [30]

There were a few pragmatic interpretations of kan by the
educated class and Buddhist monks, such as Bhikkhu Ananda
Metteyya and Bhikkhu U Thittila. According to them, kan
conveys three basic things: performance of the action, effect
of the past action and the present as the effect of the past
action. [31] The action emanates from the individual actor,
rather than from the universal and impersonal law of karma
as such. As B. U Thittila commented:

Karma, though it activates the chain of cause and
effect, is not determinism, nor is it an excuse for
fatalism. The past is the background against
which life goes on from moment to moment; the

past and the present influence the future. Only the
present moment exists, and the responsibility for
using the present moment for good or ill lies with
each individual. [32]

Unquestionably, such a definition of kan would not deter
the Burmese from the pursuit of worldly professions and the
improvement of one's material lot in life and society. Yet,
it is not certain whether this concept has been a de facto belief among the uneducated masses and the tradition-bound
political leaders. It is not unusual to find, even among the
articulate classes, an association of misfortune with bad kan
and vice versa.

In order not to exaggerate the role of the lay philosopher
in theological ramifications of Islamic doctrines, one should
notice that, for a long time, the Muslim ulema's stand against
the trend of modern thought was quite similar to that of the
Buddhist thanghahs in Burma. Muslim theologians made very
few comments, written or spoken, about religious reformation and the meaning of tradition in terms of accepting modern
thought from the Western world. Indeed, to the Muslim
ulema and Buddhist thanghahs alike, "The West stands for
pure materialism."[33] It has been observed that, at least in
the Arab world, the pleadings of the political elite to the ulema
for the acceptance and spread of modern knowledge of science
were abortive. [34] Yet in the history of Islamic religious
thought, there were various reform movements, such as the
Wahhabi and the Council of Ulema of al-Azhar in 1941, to
indicate the emergence of modernism. The same cannot be
said for Buddhism in Burma, which, until independence, received very little lay attention for modernization and reformation. Even under the leadership of highly traditional and pious
U Nu, Buddhism and its Sixth Great Buddhist Council (May,
1954) represented a revival of traditions and traditional dogmas
and not a rejection of religious thought as it existed.

In Pakistan or Muslim India, a long tradition of higher
education of a Western type, along with intense rivalry and
interchange of ideas between Islam and Hinduism, had weakened
the orthodox hold on religious thought. With respect to the
role of laymen and the educated class in the religious reformation of Islam in India, H. A. R. Gibb observed: "The more
advanced modernism of India is thus, in the main, a lay movement led by officials, lawyers, propertied men, and university
teachers, in opposition to the conservative ulema and Sufi
orders."[35]

The basic tension within the Islamic religion, social
structure and traditions in the social setting of India's caste
system introduced socioeconomic and political elements into
religious thought, thereby making Muslim India open and
congenial to the penetration of modern Western thought. By
contrast, there was no equivalent conflict between the lay and
clerical orders in colonial Burma. Both stood together against
Western intrusion under the unifying aspect of religion. It
was only after independence that tension began to develop between the tradition-bound and modernized political elites.

To be sure, the political leaders of Muslim India and
Pakistan have been exposed more to modernism, not only
through a long tradition of Western education in British India
but also through actual training and learning abroad. From
Sayyid Ahmad to General Ayub Khan, the successive leaders
of Pakistan have had some formal education and training in
the Western world. Of course, the nationalist movement in
colonial Burma was as much the work of Western-trained
political leaders (Maung Gyi, Ba Maw and others) as that of
Thakins. [36] But, on the whole, Thakins were trained and
educated at home. The psychological and philosophical congeniality or aversion to Western thought--capitalism, in
particular--of Pakistani and Burmese political leaders may
be explained by this simple parameter of exposure to Western
value systems, thought and culture. For it is through social
exposure and contact that acculturation occurs. Paradoxical
as it may seem, Burmese aversion to capitalism and Westerners was born out of a lesser contact with the Western
world and its culture.

Islamic Socialism Versus Buddhist Socialism

Scrutiny of the official philosophy and outlook on the role
of tradition and religion in Pakistan and Burma reveals, at
once, a contrasting spirit of outward-looking with inward-
looking, or more correctly, an open versus a closed society.
The modernized political elites of Pakistan seem to be able
to reconcile traditional Islamic concepts with modern thought
much more effectively than tradition-bound Burmese political
leaders. The ideologies of Pakistani leaders reflect, consistently, a successful adjustment between the traditional concept of ijma and the modern notion of volante general, the
traditional command of ceaseless endeavor (ijtehad) with the
modern concept of a religious calling found in Protestant ethics

while, at the same time, relating modern democratic ideals
to the Koran's emphasis on the oneness of humanity. At least
in the philosophical and ideological realm, modernized political
leaders in Pakistan have been able to draw broader social
groups into the central institutions of Muslim society. [37] By
contrast, tradition-bound Burmese political leaders have attempted, with very little success, to diffuse socialist and
Marxist ideologies, while, at the same time, reconciling
traditional Buddhist concepts of greed (loba) and impermanency
with those of modern socialist ideals; the results have been
rather frustrating.

This certainly does not mean that the form of government
and the actual political structure in Pakistan have been models
of democratic achievement; it does mean, however, that
Pakistan's leaders have definitely come to accept the limitations of the traditional social system as part of the normal
and desirable process in the building of a modern nation. The
most interesting contrast in official outlook toward modernization in the two countries lies in the willingness to pay the cultural price for modernization. Although both nations have
been dedicated to the preservation of traditional heritages of
Islam and Buddhism, actual policies of socioeconomic change
reflect different intensities of traditionalism. While the
Pakistani development policies of an evolutionary approach
have been consistent with the goal of preserving Islamic traditions, the Burmese ways to socialism have been less successful in adopting radical measures of economic change that would
resurrect the lost traditional society. The invocation of
traditional heritages and religions might not have been less
in Pakistan in uniting the Muslim society but the attitudes and
outlooks of its leaders seem more pragmatic than those of the
Burmese leaders.

Pakistan's Ideological Achievement

As the journalist Z. A. Suleri wrote and believed: "A
past civilization cannot be resurrected in the present time,
because in terms of modern development it is out of date; it
belongs to the past; it has minimal pull for the future. "[38]
This trend of modern thought is not really new to Pakistan,
since it is in the tradition of Mohammad Iqbal and Ayyid Khan.
As Premier Liaquat Ali Khan said, in 1950:

We have pledged that the State shall exercise its
power and authority through the chosen representa-
tives of the people. In this we have kept steadily

before us the principles of democracy, freedom,
equality, tolerance and social justice as enunciated
by Islam.   There is no room here for theocracy,
for Islam stands for freedom of conscience, con-
demns coercion, has no priesthood and abhors the
caste system. [39]

Remembering that this ideological achievement in modern
ization is not necessarily the real achievement of Pakistan in
concretizing Islamic ideals of equality and freedom, at least
the secular tendency of political thought and action is more
than apparent.   Premier Khan's firm stand against the various
demands of traditionalists and orthodox ulemas for Islamizatio
of the polity stood as witness to the spirit of secularism and
modernity with which he and his successors have resolved
traditionalism to meet the challenge of modernization.
     The same modern spirit is reflected in the official speech
of ex-President Ayub Khan, who, in speaking of the responsibility of the state, said that "it owes a singular and specific
duty to its people" and that "the essence of Tauhid ['Unity of
God'] as a working idea of equality, solidity and freedom"
is the testimony of Iqbal. [40]   The term "Islamic socialism, "
for instance, used almost interchangeably with "a modern
welfare state"[41] by the government of Pakistan, contains a
heavy emphasis on individual freedom and private incentives.
The planners of the Third Five-Year Plan stated:

Our approach to economic planning has been pragmatic all along.   It has been the constant endeavor
of the government to mobilize the creative energies
of the nation and to give all possible incentives for
the stimulation of private incentives. . . . There have
been no grand experiments in nationalization, no
fancy slogans about socialism, no undue intervention with the private sector. [42]

Although the willingness of the Pakistani political leadership to pay a cultural price for modernization may be deemed
greater than that of the Burmese socialist leadership, the approach to development in Pakistan has been consistently evolu
tionary.   With respect to the process of development and
modernization, development planners viewed its essence as
follows:

Economic development always entails profound
social changes, the speed of which varies according

to the attitudes of the community and its political
leadership toward change. It can be brought about
by a radical revolution or a slower evolutionary
manner. Pakistan has adopted the latter in order
to avoid excessive hardships and possible errors
of radicalism. [43]

In all these official positions, one can detect a pragmatic
and moderate philosophy. The welding of various religious
and spiritual ideals into modern statecraft has been successful in Pakistan by virtue of the Islamic social and political
structure, as well as by its societal openness toward the absorption of advanced alien technology and capital. As this
juncture, it will be appropriate to analyze and appraise the
official philosophy of the successive socialist governments
of the Union of Burma.

Burma's Ideological Failure

At the outset, it should be noted that despite a persistent
reluctance to pay a cultural price for modernization, the
Burmese approach to economic development has been radical
in adopting, at first, a model welfare state with a heavy emphasis on socialization, and, more recently, a Sino-Soviet
model based upon extreme Marxist ideologies. Although it
seems quite peculiar and contradictory to adopt, simultaneously,
cultural conservatism and economic radicalism, to the nationalist socialist leaders modern socialist ideals and traditional
Buddhist values are mutually compatible. This compatibility,
however, must not be taken to mean that Marxism has been
accepted as a superior philosophy to Buddhism or that its
spiritual values have been seen to offer the ultimate means
and goals of social existence. [44] In the entire political history
of Burma, one finds a persistent clash of views on the compatibility of Marxism and Buddhism, with the net result of an
eventual triumph of Buddhism.
To begin with, the entry of Marxism into Burma in the
early 1930s was based upon antimaterialistic and nationalist
forces under the direct influence of Buddhism. The political
organizations of colonial Burma under various leaders were
formed with religious overtones, which were tuned to Marxist
ideals of liberating the poor and the have-nots. The Sinyetha
Party of Ba Maw and the Wunthanu Party represented a Marxist
political twist of traditionalism, through their symbolic denunciation of the rich and the capitalist system. [45]

The Buddhist disapproval of the monetary world (ngwe
lawka) took its political form in the Marxist denunciation of
capitalism. Many popular songs of the 1930s, the "Red
Dragon, " for instance, were overlaid with the moral evils
and ills of the monetary world. Socialist literature and
Marxist ideology were read and absorbed by the articulate
political groups--Thakins and students at Rangoon University,
in particular. The acceptance of Marxism among the Thakins
was by no means unanimous; the condemnation of Marxism
as anti-Buddhist by both lay and clerical writers was quite
common.

The basic conflict of views on the compatibility of Marxism
and Buddhism has continued throughout the independent period.
Until 1962, the acceptance of Marxism and socialism by U Nu,
U Ba Swe and U Kyaw Nyein was secondary to their belief in
the all-embracing and immutable tenets of Buddhism. The
religiosity of U Nu and his tradition-bound personality tri-
umphed over radical Marxists and Communists, indicating
the nature of Burma's search for ideological identity in
Buddhism. U Nu held this concept of humanity and its short-
comings in the light of Buddhist concepts:

> Humanity has been led astray by three evils--greed,
> hatred and ignorance. Whether we are Buddhists,
> Hindus, Muslims, Christians, Animists or Atheists,
> we cannot escape the three inevitables: old age,
> disease and death. No body can deny that the five
> sense objects, viz. , pretty sight, delightful sound,
> fragrant smell, savory taste and nice touch are only
> fleeting phenomena. They are neither lasting nor
> permanent. Nobody can deny that property is transi-
> tory; no one can carry away his or her property
> after death. [46]

Indeed, these observations are made directly in terms of a
Buddhist philosophy of life, which professes that the pursuit
of worldly things is the cause of suffering and of a perpetual
circling in the whirlpool of samsara (cycle of rebirth). [47]

U Nu further discourses on the process of economic change
stating that "once upon a time all commodities were common
property and everybody had the right to use them for his or
her benefit. "[48] Since the advent of the profit motive and
capitalism, commodities became objects of exploitation. In
the classic Marxian interpretation of history, he explains the
dual class structure of haves and have-nots and the theory of

exploitation. Ultimately, the advent of the profit motive is construed to be the cause of all evils in the world. This blend-ing of Buddhism and Marxism might not have been a concrete achievement in instilling socialism in the minds of the masses; yet, the personal impact of U Nu's religious philosophy on the tradition-bound masses has been great.

From the invocation of traditionalism through various ceremonial activities--building a World Peace Pagoda, holding the Sixth Buddhist Synod, freeing 602 land and water animals and sacrificial offerings to the nats[49]--to the launching of a Pyidawtha Plan, Marxism and socialism occupied a lower plane in the official ideology of U Nu's Government. Although these activities, designed to revive traditionalism, were not totally approved by more articulate social groups in urban areas, the endorsement of the tradition-bound masses was complete. Evidence for this is found in the sweeping victory of U Nu in the 1960 election. The philosophy of development has been more traditional than modern, more Buddhistic than Marxist in Burma.

U Nu and the planners of a Pyidawtha stated: "The new Burma sees no conflict between religious values and economic progress. Spiritual health and material well-being are not enemies; they are natural allies."[50] This idealism, of course, has not been a reality in the history of development planning in Burma. For the impact of reviving traditions by means of socialism spelled the death knell for U Nu--despite his per-sonal popularity, attributed to his being an unselfish and pious leader, a man of moral integrity--[51] by creating social con-flict and mobility of certain politically and economically power-ful groups--military elites, in particular.

The glaring defect of the traditional cultural solution to the modern problem of development was its ineffectual social change. Cultural homogeneity in terms of a common religion has not served as an effective deterrent to the emergence of local nationalism and subcultural groups with new political and economic ambitions. The very traditional institutions and value systems that U Nu helped to revive and the programs of modernization that he launched under the Pyidawtha Plan came into direct conflict.

From the newspapers' political satires and cartoons of U Nu with a rosary in his hands to the private political dis-cussions of the students and intelligentsia, dissatisfaction with the use of religion for political purposes became apparent. (This was a de facto reflection of the intergeneration and intra-generation and intragroup conflict in the process of moderniza-tion.) The pillar of morality, as one of the five main pillars

of strength for Burma's modern nationhood of which U Nu so
ardently spoke, * collapsed within articulate sociopolitical
groups. [52] The principle of alternative costs in social change,
or the fact that modernization demands alteration and displace
ment of traditional institutions, was not fully understood by
U Nu and his followers.   The very students and other in-
dividuals--including military personnel--who were sent abroad
under an extensive system of state scholarships and grants,
came back to Burma with different values and outlooks from
which Burma so rigorously tried to insulate itself.   U Nu's inability to reconcile traditionalism and socialism is a classic
example of the dilemma of social change confronting many
traditional societies, some of which--Pakistan for one--are
able to resolve better than others.

Although in form and certain state socioeconomic actions,
the present philosophy of the Burmese Way to Socialism seems
somewhat radical and modern, the basic dilemmas of social
change and closing of the social system persist.   The opening
pages of the official manifesto reveal the same frustrating attempt to fuse Marxism into the Buddhist philosophical system.
In defining a true socialist economy as the one in which "participation of all for the general well-being in the works of
common ownership, and planning towards self-sufficiency and
'contentment' of all, sharing the benefits therefrom," the
traditional Buddhist emphasis of controlling desire and greed
by being content with what one has (yaunye tintain) appears
under the garb of Marxist collectivism. [53] The Burmese Way
to Socialism proclaims:

> It does not believe that so long as there exist de-
> generate systems of unfair profit-seeking, man can
> free himself from all human sufferings (dokkas).   It
> believes that unless we can build an equitable system
> with no exploitation of man by man, we cannot hope
> to reach a great new world (lawka thitkyee), which
> will free the people of all races and religions from
> such sufferings as shortage of food, clothing,
> shelter and inability to meditate due to an unfilled
> stomach, of health and happiness for mind (nama)
> and body (rupa). [54]

---

*The five pillars of strength mentioned by U Nu are the
pillars of morality, culture, economy, education and health.

Upon reading the various socialist proclamations of the Revolutionary Council Government, one perceives an uneasy sense of contradiction between two extremes: radicalism in economic change, typifying the Burmese cultural trait of deep anxiety, and stress on intention and conservatism in cultural change, characterizing the traditional tendency of being inward-looking.* This is reflected in the very name of "the Burmese Way to Socialism," which contains more alien Marxist doctrines than Burmese innovational philosophy on the ideological level. It also embodies rigorous abuses of capitalism, which are discordantly tuned to traditional cultural values in the institution of a modern socialist economy. Abuses of cutthroat capitalism, private property and profit-motivation are exposed and explained through traditional Buddhist concepts of suffering, greed and immorality of business enterprises and modern conduct (deviation from thila).[55] Marxist theses of historical social change, dialectical materialism, and economic interpretation of history and class struggle are directly used to explain the sociopolitical and economic history of Burma under the cloak of impermanency (anate-sa) and the Buddhist metaphysical concept of the world of being (loka). The best example of this curious attempt to incorporate Marxism into Buddhism can be found in the Law of Correlation (Innya Manya), which asserts:

In any case, whatever the beginning of man might be the history of society is but the history of bodily, verbal, and mental activities, in all the three periods of time, the past, the present and the future, of man in whom Rupa and Nama (matter and mind) exist as correlates.[56]

Before such a conclusion, however, the proponents of this law had already postulated a priori that "the flux of mind depends on his [man's] aggregate of matter; his mind cannot exist without this aggregate of matter on which it must continually depend."[57] This classic Marxian psychology is stretched

---

*For example, a Burmese folksaying reads "saitthah shinsaw payarhaw," meaning what counts the most is the mind or intention according to the preaching of Buddha. This belief is reflected in my discussion with many Burmese who show willingness to forgive the mistakes of the past and present governments by emphasizing the leaders' good intentions and motives.

further to explain the generic causality of man in contradiction
to the traditional concept of the importance of "the spiritual
life of the past and the present periods."[58] On the whole,
therefore, the present Burmese Way to Socialism is not essentially different from that of the previous government in
being more traditional than modern, except for its greater
endorsement of Marxian theses.

International Relations and Conflicts Affecting
Development Policies of Burma and Pakistan

Having examined the various aspects of societal closed-
ness or openness of Burma and Pakistan, the last (but not the
least) important factor relates to the contemporary setting of
international relations and conflicts that contribute directly
to the development ideologies and policies of the two countries
The degree of openness of the Pakistani social system involves
the contemporary setting of its international relations, particularly with India. From the very outset, Pakistan came into
being in direct conflict with, and indignation toward, India,
and the development planning in Pakistan derives much vigor
from the wish to be a nation distinct from its rival neighbor.
Such motivation has been reflected in the official statements
and outlook of Pakistani leaders. General Ayub Khan spoke
on Pakistan's foreign policy as follows:

> History has placed us in the pathway of the conflicting
> interests of major powers. Our location gives us a
> strategic significance both in South-East Asia and in
> the Middle East. But the cause of our major prob-
> lems is India's inability to reconcile herself to our
> existence as a sovereign, independent State.[59]

The tension and conflict of Pakistan with India has served
as the main source of political alliance with the West and of
adoption of a mixed economy of advanced capitalism. The
official slogans of the evolutionary approach to development--
no undue intervention with the market mechanism and the
private sector and no grand experiments in nationalization--
may be taken as indicators of Pakistan's desire to be quite
different from its giant neighbor. A Pakistani economist is
of the opinion that "underdeveloped countries are not to catch
up with developed ones but they are in an economic race with
each other"[60]--India in competition with China and Pakistan,
for example.

To indicate the demonstration effect among the LDCs themselves, he further contends that the formulation of the five-year plans in Pakistan has been influenced by the methods, goals and achievements of planning in India, especially the mistakes she made.[61] I should like to add that the development ideologies and policies of Pakistan, within the spectrum of international conflict, are formulated in a mood of anger and indignation against India. The truth of the demonstration effect among the LDCs themselves may also be applied to Burma, whose nationalist socialist leaders have been quick and ready to point out the social ills, cultural deterioration and political corruption of those countries that are friendly and open to the West (Thailand, for instance).

Burma's policy of societal insulation is also influenced by the impact of the Cold War and by the incidents of bipolar confrontation in Southeast Asia and elsewhere. The emergence of Red China and the ensuing flight of the Chinese Nationalist troops (Kuomingtang) inside Burma's borders, for example, led to a rapid deterioration of Burma's relations with the United States. The fact that Burma is sandwiched between the two largest countries of Asia--China and India--together with its historical experience of massive immigration of Chinese and Indians, is more than sufficient to explain Burma's policy of neutralism. In addition, recent conflicts in Korea, the Himalayan Border areas, Vietnam, the Sino-Burmese riot in the summer of 1967 and other border disputes deepened the traditional fear of potential alien intrusion.

These external events help to explain the consistent foreign policy of neutralism followed by both the civilian and military governments of Burma, which have felt the whole cultural and political survival of Burma to be at stake. The same factors are responsible for apparent contradictions in domestic political ideologies and the economic philosophy of the Burmese governments. In spite of the ideological commitment to socialism and, most recently, to the Sino-Soviet ideology of development, there has never been any significant reconciliation between the government and the underground Socialists or Communists. Burma's friendliness to China, a policy pursued throughout the independent era, has not spilled over toward internal Communists--testifying to the fact that traditional nationalism and power politics still supersede any formal commitment to a particular "ism" as such.

Recent developments in foreign policy and political ideologies in Pakistan also confirm the importance of the Cold War and the role played by the major powers, the United States,

in particular. Increased emphasis on the goal of political
and economic independence in Pakistan, along with an emphasi
on neutralism and Islamic socialism, are direct results of
the Sino-Indian conflict of 1962 and the prolonged tension between Pakistan and India, Kashmir, and so forth.

Despite a historic affinity with the West, reinforced by
anti-Communist elements in the Islamic religion of Pakistan
and the personality of Western-trained military leaders, the
rise of anti-Westernism and neutralism in recent years is
conditioned by a set of external factors, among which the
Western strategy and policy of strengthening India seem most
conspicuous to Pakistanis. Z. A. Suleri wrote about this,
stating: "For the common man of Pakistan, the surest test
of a correct Pakistani foreign policy is quite simple: does it
or does it not strengthen the country to meet and match India's
aggressive design?"[62] Suleri also listed the following factors
as contributing toward the rise of neutralism and anti-
Westernism: the lukewarm reaction of the United States towar
the Central Treaty Organization; the Dullesian edict on neutra
ism; a Five-Year Armament Plan for India, born out of the
Sino-Indian conflict; and the pro-Indian approach of solving
the question of defending the Indian subcontinent.[63]

Just as the love for neutralism in Pakistan springs from
hate for India, Burma's neutralism derives its main vigor
from its historic antipathy toward the West. The four principles of neutralism advanced by U Nu were the following: (a)
to support or object to any matter on its own merit, (b) to
establish very cordial relations with other nations whenever
possible, (c) to accept assistance to create a welfare state,
provided no strings are attached or influences demanded and
(d) to render assistance to other countries who need it.[64]
Although, in theory, the Revolutionary Council Government
pledged to follow the neutralism of previous governments, the
actual neutralism of the Burmese Way to Socialism has been
more negative than positive in foreign relations. As the
Revolutionary Council stated: "It will establish its own course
of actions and policies via self-introspection for development;
and that since it has seen the leftist and rightist inclinations
in world affairs, it will avoid such inclinations in actions."[65]

This position, of course, has not been maintained in the
vehement adoption of Marxist ideologies and state socioeconomic actions designed after the Sino-Soviet model of a
command economy. The policy of total insulation of the
Burmese society from what the Revolutionary Council termed
"the dissemination of foreign culture and propaganda" may

seem quite successful as a hermit's existence. In terms of
ideological inclinations, however, the Burmese Way to Socialism is an embodiment of alien influence reflecting the international mobility of cultures and political ideologies. Indeed,
ideological neutrality is a myth in international politics, inasmuch as the development of a nation in complete physical
isolation is a Utopian dream. Thus, ideologies and policies
of development in Burma and Pakistan are inevitably linked
to internal and external social conflict, where political and
cultural nationalism reigns supreme in the face of threats to
independence, value systems and cultures. This tendency
has certainly been stronger in Burma, by virtue of its cultural
homogeneity, traditions and historical experiences.

NOTES

1. See, for details, D. N. Wilber, Pakistan: Its People,
Its Society, Its Culture (New Haven, Conn.: Human Relations
Area Files Press, 1964), chap. 7; also, M. Mujeeb, The
Indian Muslims (Montreal: McGill University Press, 1967),
chap. iii.

2. See S. Tachibana, The Ethics of Buddhism (London:
Oxford University Press, 1926), chap. v; also, Narada Thera,
"Outline of Buddhism," The Light of the Dhamma, XI, 2
(Rangoon: Union of Burma Sasana Council, 1954), 9-12.

3. See Reuben Levy, The Social Structure of Islam
(Cambridge: Cambridge University Press, 1965), chap. i;
also, Wilber, op. cit., pp. 117-18.

4. R. V. Weeks, Pakistan: Birth and Growth of a Muslim
Nation (New York: D. Van Nostrand Co., 1964), p. 167.

5. Cf. J. A. Schumpeter, Capitalism, Socialism and
Democracy (New York: Harpers, 1962), p. 22.

6. D. E. Smith, Religion and Politics in Burma (Princeton,
N. J.: Princeton University Press, 1965), chap. 9; also, E.
E. Hagen, The Economic Development of Burma (Washington,
D. C.: The National Planning Association, 1956), pp. 7-14.

7. Lucien W. Pye, Politics, Personality, and Nation-
Building: Burma's Search for Identity (New Haven, Conn.:
Yale University Press, 1962), chap. 13.

8. Gustav Papanek, Pakistan's Development: Social
Goals and Private Incentives (Cambridge, Mass.: Harvard
University Press, 1967), p. 48.

9. See Theodore Morgan, "The Economic Development
of Ceylon," The Annals, CCCV (1956), 96.

10. Ibid., p. 47.

11. W. E. Moore, Social Change (Englewood Cliffs, N. J.:
Prentice-Hall, 1963), pp. 231-33.

12. See, for details, K. W. Jones, "Communalism in
Punjab: The Araya Samja Contribution," The Journal of
Asian Studies, XXVIII, 1 (November, 1968), 39-43.

13. See Mujeeb, op. cit., chap. vi.

14. See H. A. R. Gibb, Modern Trends in Islam (Chicago:
University of Chicago Press, 1947), pp. 13-16.

15. Z. A. Suleri, Pakistan's Lost Years: Being a Survey
of a Decade of Politics (1948-58) (Karachi: Progressive Pape
Ltd., 1962), chap. 1.

16. See Smith, op. cit., pp. 81-84.

17. See Weeks, op. cit., pp. 22-23.

18. Ibid., p. 27.

19. See U Htin Aung, "Folk Elements in Burmese
Buddhism," The Atlantic Monthly, CCI, 2 (February, 1958).

20. Levy, op. cit., p. 89.

21. Ibid.

22. See N. A. Sheikh, Some Aspects of the Constitution
and the Economics of Islam (England: The Working Muslim
Mission and Literary Trust, 1961), pp. 12-16.

23. See Levy, op. cit. , Introduction.

24. See, for details, Mya Maung, "Cultural Values and Economic Changes in Burma," Asian Survey, IV, 3 (March, 1964). Burmese folklore asserts, for example, that sales-men (zaythe) and dancers (zat-thama) are alike in their cunningness.

25. W. A. Lewis, The Theory of Economic Growth (Home-wood, Ill. : R. D. Irwin, Inc. , 1955), pp. 24-29.

26. Ibid. , p. 29.

27. See for details, W. K. Smith, Modern Islam in India (London: Victor Gollancz Ltd. , 1946), chap. 3.

28. Quoted by Smith, ibid. , p. 107.

29. From his Six Lectures on the Reconstruction of Re-ligious Thought in Islam; see Smith, op. cit. , p. 106.

30. Bhikkhu Ananda Metteyya, The Religion of Burma (Madras: Theosophical Publishing House, 1929), pp. 409-31.

31. Ibid. , p. 413.

32. Bhikkhu U Thittila, "The Meaning of Buddhism, " The Atlantic Monthly, CCI, 2 (February, 1958), p. 143.

33. Gibb, op. cit. , p. 48.

34. Ibid. , p. 50.

35. Ibid. , p. 57.

36. See, for details, Maung Maung Pye, Burma in the Crucible (Madras: The Diocesan Press, 1951).

37. See Suleri, op. cit. , pp. 11-13; also, cf. S. N. Eisenstadt, Modernization: Protest and Change (Englewood Cliffs, N. J. : Prentice Hall, 1966), p. 52.

38. Suleri, op. cit. , p. 11.

39. Liaquat Ali Khan, Pakistan: The Heart of Asia (Cambridge, Mass. : Harvard University Press, 1951), p. 6.

40. Mohammad Ayub Khan, Pakistan Perspective (Washir ton, D. C. : Embassy of Pakistan, 1965), p. 4.

41. Outline of the Third Five-Year Plan. . . , p. v.

42. Ibid. , p. iv.

43. Ibid. , p. v.

44. See J. S. Thomson, "Marxism in Burma, " F. N. Trager, ed. , Marxism in Southeast Asia (Stanford, Calif. : Stanford University Press, 1959), pp. 46-50.

45. Cf. F. R. von der Mehden, Religion and Nationalism in Southeast Asia (Madison: The University of Wisconsin Press, 1963), p. 71.

46. U Nu, Forward with the People (Rangoon: Ministry o Information, 1955), p. 28.

47. Ibid.

48. Ibid. , p. 29.

49. See Smith, op. cit. , chap. 5.

50. Pyidawtha: The New Burma (London: Hazel Watson & Viney Ltd. , 1957), p. 10.

51. Smith, op. cit. , p. 141; also, Hugh Tinker, The Unio of Burma (London: Oxford University Press, 1959), p. 117.

52. U Nu, Burma Looks Ahead (Rangoon: Ministry of In- formation, 1953), pp. 1-3.

53. The Philosophy of the Burma Socialist Programme Party: The System of Correlation of Man and His Environmer (Rangoon: Ministry of Information, 1963), pp. 44-47. (Here- after cited as System of Correlation . . . .)

54. Translated from the Burmese text of The Burmese Way to Socialism (Rangoon: Revolutionary Council, 1962).

55. System of Correlation . . . , pp. 44-47.

56. Ibid., p. 38.

57. Ibid., p. 3.

58. Ibid., p. 15.

59. Mohammad Ayub Khan, Friends Not Masters: A Political Autobiography (New York: Oxford University Press, 1967), p. 115.

60. Mahbubul Haq, The Strategy of Economic Development: A Case Study of Pakistan (Karachi: Oxford University Press, 1963), p. 9.

61. Ibid., p. 10.

62. Z. A. Suleri, Politicians: Being A Survey of Pakistani Politics from 1948-1964 (Lahore: Lion Art Press, 1966), p. 152.

63. Ibid., pp. 151-55.

64. Burma Looks Ahead, op. cit., p. 103.

65. The Burmese Way to Socialism (in Burmese), op. cit., p. 12.

CHAPTER 5   ECONOMIC POLICY,
MEASURES AND
RESPONSES

Since the military take over of political power, economic
policy in Burma and Pakistan has changed. In Burma, this
has taken the much more drastic form of a complete switch
from an evolutionary to a revolutionary approach toward socialism. The Revolutionary Council Government has swiftly
transformed the organizational structure of the economy from
a welfare state, with heavy emphasis on governmental control
to a command economy, with no toleration of private enterpris
Although such an approach to development is not an entirely
new experience in the history of developing economies, the
case of Burma offers a classic example of the "simple" substitution of government for private enterprise in the transfer
of ownership and control of resources from the private to the
public sector. In following an evolutionary path toward develo
ment, the military government of General Ayub Khan, on the
other hand, began to dismantle state controls in 1959, instead
of relying heavily on private incentive and the market mechani
Although the difference in economic performance of the
two countries cannot simply be attributed to the timeworn issu
of public versus private enterprise, it is also true that appropriate changes in economic policy are capable of either stimulating or retarding social incentives and the propensity to develop. At least in the LDC, where the role of the state in
promoting economic development is considered one of the mos
crucial factors, analysis of the response to specific economic
measures introduced by the ruling political elite is of the utmo
importance.
In this chapter, I shall deal with the question of the appro
priateness of economic policies in light of the sociocultural
parameters that were given before; specifically, with measure
such as trade liberalization schemes in Pakistan and total nati
alization, "advance purchase of paddy system," "demonetizati
of K.100 and K.50 notes" and "People's Stores Corporation"
in Burma. These cases show that the effectiveness of certain

118

economic measures is not a simple matter of transfer of resources from the private to the public sector and vice versa;
it is also a matter of social response and the ability of particular cultures to absorb and disseminate modern values and technology. The recent history of both Burma and Pakistan proves
that not all government economic actions are efficient and that
some of them can inhibit, rather than stimulate, economic
growth.

EQUITY VERSUS PRODUCTIVITY

To achieve the economic goals of equity in income distribution and productivity in the economy, the substitution of public
for private enterprise (or vice versa) is not only of theoretical
interest but also of strategic importance in the development-
planning LDCs. Current polemical discussions on the economic
development of LDCs invariably touch upon inequity in income
distribution as one of the features, as well as the problems,
of development. Polemics on socialism versus capitalism,
revolutionary versus evolutionary approaches to development
and balanced versus imbalanced or disequilibrium strategies
of development somehow or other pivot around the age-old issue
of state versus private ownership--of control of resources, on
the one hand, and relative roles of public and private enterprise in promoting growth, on the other.

Within this framework, Burma and Pakistan seem to fit
into two opposite patterns of development policy: in one, the
major emphasis is on a revolutionary approach and the absolute
role of the state to achieve equity; in the other, on an evolutionary approach, which makes use of the private sector to
achieve productivity. Since, in both countries, it is the state
that initiates and maintains certain economic policies, development experiences in Burma and Pakistan are not confined to
the issue of private versus public enterprise. Economic measures undertaken by the state, however, do contribute directly
to the economic performance of the two countries and to the
open or closed nature of the social system.

Equity versus productivity, like price stability versus full
employment, is still considered a classic example of a dichotomy of goals. Economic policy favoring efficiency has often
been equated with reliance on private incentives and the market
mechanism, whereas economic policy favoring equity has been
equated with public enterprise and control. This dichotomy,

however, seems less applicable to the LDCs, in view of the
fact that inequity in income distribution has been considered
one of the major obstacles to rapid development and, also,
that there is no adequate private entrepreneurial base[1]--con-
ditions that would seem to favor a strong state role in promoting economic growth.

It is certainly true that concern for distributive justice
among statesmen and politicians in the LDCs is necessary as
a symbol of moral integrity[2] and political legitimacy. Yet,
central to the problem of economic development is the fact
that an excessive concern for either equity or productivity can
lead to the adoption of inappropriate economic measures and
resulting repercussions detrimental to the goal of development.
Indeed, the conflict between efficiency and distributive equity
is much more acute in LDCs, simply because the living standard is so low, so that dividing a small economic cake among
the masses can lead to economic retardation and further im-
poverishment along with inequity.

Burma's recent experiment with a command economy of
distributive justice is a case in point. On the other hand, too
much concentration of economic power and wealth in a few individuals or families can create insurmountable social and
economic barriers for the masses in addition to their poverty.
In terms of the priorities of social and economic goals, the
Pakistani development experience offers an interesting contrast
to Burma.

It is undoubtedly true that "when it can effectively operate
the price mechanism is a very good device for interrelating
value criteria and efficiency criteria."[3] In Burma, this has
not happened, due to the lack of an indigenous entrepreneurial
base or adequate machinery and human resources to correct
market imperfections. The presence of economically power-
ful foreign Orientals and the obsession of the nationalist politi
cal leadership with the evils of capitalism have, in fact, led
to a total abandonment of the price mechanism, with disastrous
economic consequences. Pakistan, on the other hand, has
demonstrated both that the market mechanism is a useful device for promoting economic growth and that the relative neglect of equity can be politically dangerous. The argument--
that in the early stages of development one should let the size
of the economic cake grow bigger while sharing it equitably
later--seems to fit Pakistan's development policy and goals.[4]
The exact opposite is true of Burma's experiment with socialism. The paradox here, of course, is that the socioeconomic
structure of the two countries seems to call for the opposite

of the actual development strategy each has chosen. In any case, economic policy and goals in LDCs do arise out of the complex social and political settings and motivations of the dominant political elites.

As stated earlier, the priority given to productivity and private incentives in the development planning of Pakistan is a function of the value-orientation, outlook and personality of its political leadership. The personal background of successive political leaders--and the military elite, in particular--has been such that the goal of ideal distributive equity remains sub-servient to efficiency and pragmatic planning in Pakistan. In this respect, observers have said of General Ayub Khan: "Most of his life Ayub had proved an optimistic yet constructively pragmatic realist, unimpressed by the abstract or theoretical, undemonstrative but compelling, considerate where possible but ruthless when necessary..."[5]

To what extent such a personality has influenced the de-velopment policy and goals of Pakistan may be hard to measure, yet the spirit and thought of the entire Third-Year Plan reflects pragmatism and realism. The basic priority given to produc-tivity over income and regional equity can be discerned in vari-ous symposia on developmental planning in Pakistan. The per-sonality of political leaders alone, of course, is not responsible for this. For the emergence and popularity of certain types of political personalities are equally the product of the social and historical environment of a country at any given time.[6] In Pakistan, it happened that the British-trained civil service and military elite came to dominate the polity.

Under the political rule and management of the civil service and, later, the military government, the goal of distributive equity has been given symbolic attention as a political necessity. The actual measures of economic reform have been aimed at stimulating productivity and private incentives. Despite the land and agrarian reforms introduced by various governments, large landholdings of up to 500 acres (irrigated) or 1,000 acres (unirrigated)--a government ceiling--had been permitted in West Pakistan. Through deeding of land to relatives, however, many large landlords have been able to maintain control, thereby circumventing the ceiling.[7] In East Pakistan, the breaking up of Hindu Zaminders' control of the land was accomplished soon after partition, when the government limited landholding to thirty-three acres per family. Yet, the family lineage system and the power of traditional landlords have led to continued control of the land and of rural economic life. Indeed, the economic policy of what G. Papanek termed "squeezing the

peasant" might have been effective in mobilizing private industrial savings and increasing productivity. Instead, it has
produced regional disparities in income distribution, on the
one hand, and in the relative pace of industrialization, on the
other, between East and West Pakistan.

Exact statistical data on the distributive equity of income
are not available. It may be inferred, however, that priority
given to productivity has repercussions in the stagnant real
income of the rural poor in Pakistan and the sociopolitical rift
between the industrially powerful West and the predominantly
agricultural East. As S. R. Bose observed, "There is little
doubt that the fall in per capita income of the agricultural population during the 1950s has not been made good by the slight
reversal observed in 1963-64."[8] Fall in per capita income
of the rural poor and increased urban-rural disparity of economic growth in Pakistan indirectly reflect the problem of
distributive equity within each of its segments and the regional
disparity in sharing the national economic cake. In 1964-65,
for example, the disparity ratio of per capita income between
the West and East was given as 1:34, i.e., the ratio of Rs.
547.9 (West) to Rs. 377.1 (East).[9] The "squeezing" of agriculture and the peasants, brought about by industrial development in Pakistan--and the West, in particular--has had serious
social and political consequences in recent years.

Reliance on private enterprise and the market mechanism
in the development strategy of Pakistan has been based upon
the assumption that a high rate of economic growth is a direct
function of a high rate of savings, which, in turn, is a direct
function of the growth of the capitalist sector. The basic be-
havorial postulate is that capitalists have a high propensity to
save. The implication of this assumption is concentration of
income and wealth in the hands of the high savers who would
be given maximum advantages and incentives to invest. The
result of such a policy of development in Pakistan has been
observed to produce monopolies and concentration of economic
power in the industrial sector. As a Pakistani economist remarked: "Nowhere else in the world, except perhaps Germany
have the industrial 'robber barons' been fed such large chunks
of 'meat' at the expense of public exchequer."[10]

Various fiscal measures taken to stimulate private incentives were a differential tax in favor of dividends--10 percent
for the corporate rate of 45 percent--a rebate of personal income tax for investment up to 40 percent, a tax holiday of four
to eight years, an export bonus and special privileges in forei
trade and other tax exemptions.[11] These, plus other liberali
zation measures, have undoubtedly created a favorable busine

climate for the industrial capitalists. What becomes uncertain
in such an effort is the thesis of a high propensity to save on
the part of the industrial capitalists. A number of studies seem
to suggest that this assumption of development policy-makers
has not been quite correct, and that the price of trade-off between more equitable distribution of income and maximization
of savings has been very high for Pakistan.[12]

In the 1950s, a few families with an industrial background--
the Saigols, Adamjee, Dawoods, and so forth--came to dominate the entire industrial sector under the open general license
policy of the government. The same has been observed for
the 1960s. R. H. Khandher, for example, observed that "though
no individual or group has a dominant role in trade and commerce, the business is however limited to a great extent within
a few communities like the Memons, the Bohras and the
Kojas."[13] He further observed that 90 percent of the inter-
wing trade was controlled by the Memons, who also controlled
60 percent of foreign imports into Karachi and Chittagong. In
1968, it was estimated that about twenty families controlled
66 percent of Pakistan's industrial assets, 70 percent of its
insurance funds and 80 percent of its bank assets.[14]

G. Papanek may be quite correct in his argument that state
controls and price regulations in the 1950s were the cause of
a depressed agriculture in Pakistan and that "Pakistani peasants
do act, to a considerable extent, as rational economic men"
in their responses to price incentive schemes of the government during the 1960s.[15] What remains essentially critical
and uncertain, however, is the relative contributions of industrial capitalists and rural agriculturalists to capital formation, on the one hand, and their relative shares of the economic
cake, on the other. As one economist has observed, "Economic
policy pursued in Pakistan involved a huge redistribution of
income between rural and urban sectors. The contribution of
this income transfer to real saving is far short of the burden
of saving imposed on the rural sector."[16] Such a method of
intersectoral intermediation is considered weak because of
the high spill-over effect, the divorce of savings from their
rewards and the adverse effects on the allocation of resources
and growth of financial intermediaries.

From these observations, it may be concluded that the
efficiency-oriented development policy of Pakistan has paid
some distributive price in the form of intersectoral and inter-
wing disparities, along with sociopolitical tensions and conflicts. Although it is not quite certain as to whether or not
the spectacular growth of the Pakistani economy in the 1960s

has been due to the liberalization measures of the government,
it can be affirmed that there have been positive responses to
the state-initiated economic policy of private greed for public
benefits. The social utility of greed, properly controlled, is
a useful device for promoting economic growth, even though
the neglect of distributive justice is politically dangerous in
a country characterized by initial disparities in wealth and by
institutional rigidity with regard to social and economic mobili
     Though the Pakistani experience in development planning
by no means offers conclusive evidence of an experiment in
capitalism, the Burmese experience under its economic policy
of the Burmese Way to Socialism provides direct evidence of
an experiment with a command economy, which is unique to
the social and political environment of Burma. The obsession
of Burmese political leaders with socialism and distributive
justice seems to have reached its highest peak under the economic management of the present Revolutionary Council Gover
ment. Yet the military government's total neglect of productivity in its short-run ad hoc economic schemes since 1962 has
taken a heavy toll in economic performance. For the remaind
of this chapter, I shall analyze and evaluate specific economic
measures undertaken by the Revolutionary Council in the name
of equity and justice. The main hypothesis here will be that a
system of direct controls, like the one the military governmer
has introduced in Burma, usually breeds a vicious circle of
control-evasion-control, with the net effect of both inefficiency
and inequity.

The Burmese Experiment with a Command Economy

     Since the military coup d'état of March 2, 1962, the Revo
lutionary Council Government of the Union of Burma has wage
a relentless war against the remnants of capitalism from its
colonial heritage and the civilian government. Under the bann
of "the Burmese Way to Socialism," the military junta swiftly
transformed the organizational structure of the Burmese econ
omy from a model of democratic socialist economy to that of
a command economy within three years after the take-over of
political power. Socialization, nationalization and state controls have been so extensive that the socialist economy of the
former civilian government seems like a dwarf compared with
the giant infrastructure of governmental boards, committees,
councils and corporations of the present military government.
The general effects of such an approach to economic developm

have already been touched upon in the second chapter. More
specifically, the Revolutionary Council's experiment with a
command economy exemplifies a revolutionary approach to
economic development that has had the net effect of economic
stagnation, due to neglect of what economists consider to be
the end of economic life--the maximization of output in terms
of preferred products with a minimum of satisfaction sacri-
ficed.[18]

The transfer of resources from the private to the public
sector, as an organizational means of promoting economic
growth and correcting inequity in income distribution, is a
relatively recent phenomenon, which was born out of the Sino-
Soviet experience and experiment. Though the models of economic growth advanced by classical and neoclassical economists,
including most modern neo-Keynesians, consider the process
of income distribution and set standards and measures of distributive equity and justice, the basic postulates and social
objectives of capitalism preempt an analysis of how growth
can begin by nationalization of resources. Even in Marxian
theories of surplus value, exploitation and class struggle, this
question was indirectly tackled. Marxian economics represents
a sociopolitical critique of capitalism and its evolution, rather
than an economic analysis of the development process.[19]

The appeal of the socialist prescription of state ownership
and control of the means of production to the nationalist political
leadership of many LDCs stems from the Marxian thesis that
economic poverty of the masses, or "immiserization" of the
proletariat, is the natural outcome of capitalism. In an ex-
colony, such as Burma, this thesis becomes a source of nationalism, developmental aspirations and rationalizations for
failures in modernization. In Burma, socialism has been
chosen with the conviction that the roots of economic underdevelopment lie in an unjust economic system of capitalism,
introduced and nurtured by colonial powers of the past. Revolutionary socialism and the choice of a command economy as
the model of development was made by the Revolutionary Council
Government, which charged the previous civilian government
with betraying the true course of socialism by perpetuating the
pernicious economic system of capitalism.[20]

The major indictment of the economic policy of the civilian
government was summed up by the Revolutionary Council as
follows: "The Union was dominated by the feudalists for over
a thousand years, by the foreign imperialists for over a hun-
dred years, and was dominated by the landlords and capitalists
after it had attained independence."[21]

With regard to the reason for the continuation of Sino-India
domination of the Burmese economy, General Ne Win assessed
the problem as due partly to the pernicious economic system
of the civilian government and partly to the fact that "the
Burmese are mostly lazybones."[22] The sale of import li-
censes to the Indian and Chinese capitalists, for example, was
cited as a testament of the indigenous capitalists' infatuation
with a petit bourgeois mentality. In line with the classic
Marxian stages theory of economic development, the Revolutionary Council concluded:

> History will generally record that in the march of
> man the indigenous people of Burma lagged behind.
> When the capitalist economic system was in full
> power in the West European countries, Burma and
> similar countries slumbered in the shadow of the
> feudalist economic system.[23]

This curious explanation of Burma's economic underdevelopment and history, particularly the dominance of the bourgeois class after independence, is indicative of the intensity
of social conflict with which the entire philosophy of the Burmese Way to Socialism has been formulated. Although it is
quite true that the socialist economy of the civilian government did not carry out various socialization programs--land
nationalization, for instance--the explanation of Burma's economic history by the dominance of the bourgeois class is rather
exaggerated. For the absence of a strong middle class, administrators, entrepreneurs and managers has been the key
problem in enforcing the so-called socialist economy of proportional development by the military government.

In any case, with these theories and beliefs, the Revolutionary Council Government envisaged an ideal socialist society
as "the participation of all for the general well-being in works
of common ownership, and planning towards sufficiency and
contentment of all, sharing the benefits derived therefrom."[24]
The reasons for the military coup were given in the light of
problems confronting Burma under what the Revolutionary
Council labeled as a government with "a bourgeois Parliament."[25] The problems were identified as: (a) political splits
(b) national disunity, (c) capitalist Parliament, (d) foreign
capitalist investment, (e) corruption of culture, (f) low standard
of education and (g) poverty of peasants and workers.[26]

So much for the beliefs and theories of the Burmese Way
to Socialism. The basis for all these is to be found in the Revolutionary Council's conception of a true socialist economy:

Socialist economy proportionally plans, on the basis
of population and productive forces, for sufficiency
and abundance of consumers goods. While improv-
ing the standard of living and increasing the purchasing power of the nation, it also expands production.[27]

This growth-oriented concept of a socialist economy, combined with the image of an equitable socialist society, has led
the military government to adopt a model of a command economy,
in which the role of the state is extolled in the ownership, control and operation of all productive forces. More than seven-
teen laws on economic affairs were passed, empowering the
state to nationalize, determine prices, trade and manage the
entire economy of Burma.[28] With centralized decision-making
authority vested in the political bodies of the Revolutionary
Council and the Council of Ministers (Wungyis), the military
managers and political cadres of the BSPP thus carry out the
entrepreneurial function in agriculture, commerce, industry
and finance. Of all these laws, the 1963 Law to Protect the
Construction of the Socialist Economy, the 1963 People's
Stores Corporation Law and the 1964 Law to Protect the Construction of the Socialist Economy from Opposition are the
most pertinent for the purpose of this study. The first and the
third laws were sequential state actions in the nationalization
of banks and demonetization of K.100 and K.50 notes, while
the third gave the state a monopoly of all trade and distribution
of goods and services.*

Nationalization and Economic Stagnation

At the outset, it should be noted that the socialist economy
that has been established so far by the military government in
Burma is far from the ideals of "planned proportional development of all productive forces" and "increased purchasing power
and expanded production." In the first place, except for a
complete transfer of resources from the private to the public
sector, the Burmese economy has remained unplanned in the
modern sense of a centrally planned socialist economy.[29] It
is in this sense that the Burmese Way to Socialism may be
conceived of as truly unique to the Burmese social framework.
The actual planning and operation of various state enterprises
are done on the basis of short-lived ad hoc committees and

---

*The first and the third laws were Law No. 1 and Law
No. 7.

councils, which are created as organs of stop-gap compensa-
tory state actions in plugging the loopholes attending a system
of direct controls.

In the absence of a systematic survey of factor endowment
and production targets, the ideal of planning on the basis of
population and productive forces has very little meaning in an
underdeveloped economy such as Burma. Since 1962, whateve:
planning machinery that existed under the Eight-Year Pyidawth•
Plan (1952-60) of the U Nu Government has deteriorated, nor
has there been an improvement in the state apparatus of planning. A Socialist Economy Construction Committee of the
BSPP came into being (nominally) in 1965 and was abolished
during that same year of inactivity. [30] The former Ministry
of National Planning has so far remained inactive in the formulation of long-range plans for economic development. Similar•
the important state agency of economic and statistical survey,
the Central Statistical and Economics Department of the forme
government, has suffered a major setback in its output of information, due to changes in the power structure and the allocation of functions among newly created government agencies.

Apart from the fact that the Revolutionary Council, with
less than twenty nucleus members of the BSPP, is the locus
of power and decision-making in the formulation of major economic policies, there has not been any important state agency
of national planning that can be compared to the State Planning
Commission of either China or Russia. The major change in
the organization of the Burmese economy, therefore, lies not
in the actual structuring of a centralized planned economy as
such but in the creation of totally nationalized, centralized
state councils, committees and corporations, without any
coordinated scheme of planning and implementation.

The outstanding feature of the Burmese command economy
is its centralization of command and the displacement of civili•
entrepreneurial functions by the Special Duty Officers of Burm•
Defense Services. The former governmental agencies, such
as the State Agricultural Marketing Board and the State Timbe:
Board were renamed "Corporations" and given numbers, unde:
the new management of the Trade Council, which was, former•
the Ministry of Trade and Development. The Trade Council,
with Brigadier Tin Pe as minister, appears to be the most
important development in the management of the Burmese
economy; by creating a network of twenty-three Corporations,
some old and some new, a complete state monopoly of all trad•
and distribution was affected. Under the same ministry, the
People's Stores Corporation also became a most notorious and•

inefficient organization--a fact which the military government
itself has to admit. In the areas of finance, public works,
transportation and agriculture, former ministries and agencies
have continued to operate with little or no change in their functional modus operandi except for the change in management.

In order of priority and actual sequence, the nationalization of banks, trade, industry and business took place within
three years, from 1962 to 1965. Nationalization of banks, the
first target of the Revolutionary Council Government, was
carried out with relative ease after passing the Law to Protect
the Construction of the Socialist Economy in 1963. This became a simple matter of transforming the banking system
from one with a few private banks to one with no private banks.

To begin with, the banking system of independent Burma
was primarily governmental with respect to the flow of funds
and direct controls of foreign exchange. The Union Bank of
Burma, the State Commercial Banks and the State Agricultural
Banks have always controlled the sources of funds, while the
only important private banks that dealt with international finance
were twenty-three foreign banks. In addition, eight indigenous
private banks financed small businesses in urban areas. In
the banking system, therefore, the main target of nationalization was foreign banks. The military government renamed all
commercial banks, state and private, as People's Banks, which
became the central financial institutions for financing governmental enterprises. It should be noted that although the process of nationalizing banks was a simple matter of government
takeover, the inefficiency in implementation had led to massive
withdrawal of funds and evasion, even before the time of nationalization. Demonetization of K.100 and K.50 notes in the
following year was due precisely to the loophole through which
the leakage of the news of nationalization and the withdrawal
of funds from banks had rendered the state action ineffective.

Secondly, nationalization of all trade, business and industry has failed to engender the increased standard of living
in the nation, due to the development of a nationwide black
market, known as Corporation No. 24;[31] the decline of production as a by-product of disincentive effects and artificial
scarcity created by a system of price control and rationing;
and a concealed inflation of both demand-pulled and govern-
mentally-induced types. The development of the black market
is a direct result of nationalization and the inability of the
government to plug the loopholes.

In addition, the People's Stores, which became sole sup-
pliers of all goods, have been run primarily by civilians, whose

profit motivation has not been curbed by the Burmese Way to
Socialism. The distribution or sale of goods was made by
these stores under a quota system according to the size of the
family; sales were made on the basis of quota booklets or identification cards, which became tickets used to transfer goods
from where it was cheap to where it was dear--from government shops to the black market. If all consumers could get
their quota shares at government shops, of course, there
would be no black market. The shortage of goods at government People's Stores, thus, has been the main problem.

In this way the benevolent objectives of low prices and
equitable sharing of benefits were undermined by the profit
motives of storekeepers and consumers alike, the shortage
of goods and the resale of scarce commodities at exorbitantly
high prices in the black market. The glaring deficiency of
this governmentally administered system of pricing and distribution is revealed not only in the distortion of relative prices
but also in the maldistribution of various products. Modern
consumer goods, such as toothbrushes, toothpastes, soaps
and toilet paper, for example, were found in remote village
shops, where there was no demand for them. Also, arbitrary
pricing by the government and the artificial scarcity created
by a system of rationing resulted in a distortion of relative
price patterns.

With respect to the shortage of supply of goods in the
government stores, the major factors are the following: (a)
the unwillingness of private producers to produce and sell
their products at low prices to the only buying unit, monopso-
nist buying depots of the government, (b) the excess demand
and profit prevalent in the black market and (c) mismanagement in procurement, storage and sale. The disincentive
effect of a system of state monopsony was most devastating
in the production and export of agricultural products, which
seemed to have dwindled greatly under the military management of the economy. The supposedly novel innovation of the
Revolutionary Council Government was the introduction of "a
system of advance purchase of paddy" at a fixed low price.
With regard to this, the government proclaimed:

> The advance paddy purchase system of the Revolu-
> tionary Council had no resemblance whatsoever to
> the pintaung system of the capitalists. The pintaung
> system of the capitalists was used by them to gain
> 100 percent profit on their capital within a few
> months. The capitalists bought the standing crops

at half of what they would be worth at the time of
the harvest. The system of purchase employed by
the Revolutionary Council was procurement at the
price which would prevail at the time of harvesting. [32]

With this interesting theory on a benevolent system of the
advance purchase of paddy, the Revolutionary Council further
explained that the price which would prevail at the time of
harvesting would be for the months of December, January and
February, without specification as to how this was calculated.
As for paddy of the longer-maturity variety beyond these months,
the procurement price would remain fixed, despite the recognition that the actual harvest price would be higher. To justify
this fixed price policy irrespective of time, it was stated that
"since the peasants would have received the value of sales
without interest at an earlier date they would not lose on that
account." [33] Indeed, the new system relative to the pintaung
system would not cost interest to the cultivators; yet it remains
unconvincing how a system of fixed prices offered to the cultivators of different varieties--and of long-maturity paddy, in
particular--would represent a zero cost. Not to have to pay
a higher price for paddy of longer maturity certainly represents a zero cost to the government buying depot. For the
growers of such a crop, the net loss is real enough in terms
of the unpaid price differential or the higher cost of inputs for
a longer investment period. It makes little sense to speak of
educating the cultivators on that score[34] and on fair prices in
an economy where there is no free interplay of market forces.
Under a system of state monopsony, the concept of fair prices
remains, at best, arbitrary. To be sure, the Burmese cultivators have taken double advantage of the system by entering
a contract with the state buying depots, thereby receiving
direct agricultural loans and selling the paddy on the black
market for a phenomenal profit. Failure to deliver the con-
tracted volume has not been a serious problem, since the advance purchase system was introduced on the basis of only
five baskets per acre, or one-sixth of the average yield per
acre.
     Internal maintenance by the government of a fixed, low
price for paddy is by no means a new, revolutionary policy
of the military government. The State Agricultural Marketing
Board (SAMB) has done the same since independence. Under
previous governments, the SAMB bought paddy in the field or
at the depot at K. 2.80 or K. 3 per basket. The price differential
between these and that of private dealers was about K. 2 in

1961-62, K.5 per basket being the private offered price.[35]
Under the new system, the SAMB was renamed Corporation
No. 1 and the purchase price raised to a minimum of K.3.10
and a maximum of K.3.85 per basket.[36] The most common
offered price has been the minimum, which means a little over
3 percent increase on the fixed price. The sale price of rice
at the People's Stores, however, has been steadily going up
since 1962. The average price at these stores has increased
from K.12.80 per basket in 1963 to over K.20 per basket in
recent years. This price differential between paddy and rice
in the domestic economy and the substantially higher export
price of both paddy and rice have remained a major source of
government revenue, but in monopolizing the entire wholesale
and retail trade of paddy and rice, the price differential between the government and private black markets seems to have
skyrocketed. Although no exact statistics are available, Burmese newspaper accounts place the price of paddy in the black
market as high as K.28 per basket in the vicinity of Rangoon.[3]
From this data, one can imagine how high the black-market
price of rice and imported products would be.

What has changed most conspicuously in the rural economy
of Burma is the multiple growth and congestion of state agencies
and cooperatives. The government agencies include state buying depots, village banks, tractor stations, village shops and
local administrative bodies, known as Security Administration
Committees, which replaced the former District Commissioner
Office of the Home Ministry. The Agricultural Multi-Purpose
Cooperatives (AMPCs), formerly called Multi-Purpose Producers Cooperatives (ProCos), and Land Committees were
formed on a large scale as intermediary institutions of trade,
aid and finance under the direct vanguard of the BSPP political
cadres. Apart from these, the various agencies of ministries
persist in running the rural economy of Burma through a magnificent network of uncoordinated government enterprises.
Under the 1963 Law to Protect the Rights of Peasants and the
1965 Law to Amend the Tenancy Act of 1963, the system tenancy
and rent were abolished. These laws, plus other laws to con-
struct the socialist economy, made the government the capitalist, landlord, entrepreneur, banker and merchant, all at
once.

The growth of state buying depots of agricultural produce
was recorded as more than 250 percent between 1961 and 1965,
from 524 in 1961 to 1,457 in 1965.[38] The growth of AMPCs
and their adjunct village shops is given as over 300 percent,
from 6,731 ProCos in 1961 to over 21,000 AMPCs and village

shops in 1965. [39] It should be noted that, as far as the main functions of these cooperatives are concerned, there seems to be no essential difference from those of the former ProCos. The major functions have remained the same, both in their confinement to credit and the sale of consumer goods, the sources of which are now purely government.

The main motivation for cooperation in Burma has always been the easy procurement of credit and aid from the state, which has been boosted greatly under the more liberal credit programs of the Revolutionary Council Government. The number of village banks, for instance, increased from 2,221 in 1960-61 to 9,820 in 1964-65. The interest charged by these village banks or the State Agricultural Banks was also reduced --from 6 percent to 3 percent--together with an increase of the lending limit* from about K.30 to K.50 per acre since 1962-63. [40]

This quantitative push on the agricultural front is a natural political action in an agricultural economy such as Burma, where a Marxian "mode of production" is epitomized in the tillers of the soil rather than "the industrial reserved army of the unemployed proletariat" as such. Whatever the political motivation of the Revolutionary Council Government may be, the accelerated flow of funds from the People's Banks to the peasants may seem highly commendable with respect to the redistribution of income and reinvestment of government profit accumulated under a system of state monopoly of all trade and industry. It has been observed by some economists that SAMB's policy of a fixed low price for paddy internally under the previous government amounted to a tax on cultivators' income, and its impact on the cultivator's lot in the distribution of income was uncertain, except for the result of advancing low-interest agricultural loans. [41]

With an increase in fixed low prices for paddy, plus a multiple rate of increase in lending lower-interest cultivation loans, the cultivators' cut of the Burmese national cake seems larger under the Burmese Way to Socialism. The level of cultivation loans in 1965-66, for example, was recorded as more than ten times higher than the average annual level of K.50 million in the 1950s. Total accumulated loans, old and new, for the same year was given as over K.1 billion. [42]

---

*The limit of lending means here a general limit rather than pure cultivation loans as such. The village banks' limit on cultivation loans was K.8 per acre before 1962, which was raised to K.25 per acre in 1963.

It should be noticed, however, that the rate of return of these loans has also decreased, which indicates the misuse of funds and a state of stagnant agricultural productivity in the rural economy of Burma. The annual amount of unpaid accumulated loans has been almost equal to the annual amount of new loans advanced each year since 1962;[43] and the percent of return of newly advanced loans has averaged less than 70 percent, in contrast to over 75 percent per annum in the 1950s.[44] The same problem of accumulated arrears of agricultural loans, which forced the former government to write them off in 1961, seems to be plaguing the military government in confirming the disincentive effect of liberal credit and fixed price policies. The problem has been worse under the new economic system of state monopoly and rationing.

A simultaneous state action of pouring cash into the rural economy and controlling prices, without a concomitant rise in the supply of goods, has, naturally, produced intensive pressures of inflation in the black market. The price differential between goods sold by the government and by black markets cuts across a whole range of commodities--prices of imported goods being the highest. The price of rice in the black market has been four to five times higher than that of the government, while clothing, cooking oil and household utensils prices have been five to ten times higher.[45] The People's Stores, the AMPCs and the village shops have become the major channel of peddling goods, in the light of the government's inability to police each and every economic transaction.* In giving an artificial scarcity value to quota slips and allotment of a family's share on a purely quantitative basis, resale of goods by householders has been a common occurrence. This, of course, is the precise problem of rationing and of a global quota system, in which the distribution of goods according to needs and taste is an impossibility. Furthermore, in a traditional society, with its poor accounting method and records, where most economic affairs--inclusive of state economic actions--are run on the basis of personal relations, cultural habits and customs and cash, the task of keeping track of goods and a fungible commodity, such as cash, is impossible to perform.

---

*The stealing and black-marketeering of goods at cooperative shops are not entirely new, although they have increased rapidly under the military management. Since independence, Consumers Cooperatives (ConCos) have been sarcastically labeled as ConKhos, meaning, in Burmese, stealing of goods.

The shortage of human resources, entrepreneurs, managers and administrators and so forth and a low state of technology have been augmented by creating large-scale government projects and enterprises under the Burmese Way to
Socialism. The formal substitution of military entrepreneurs
and managers for civilian ones and of government for private
markets, without plans and rigorous implementation for production, procurement and supervision, is not only ineffective
but also repressive of agricultural productivity and growth.
A lack of economic security and freedom of choice further
chokes off the flow of innovation, while bureaucratic delays
and red tape result in inefficiency of performance. [46]

Glaring examples of inefficiency can be found in the economic waste of decay of perishable foodstuffs in the People's
Stores, leakages of goods and losses in governmental opera-
tions. The outright nationalization of wholesale and retail
trade of foodstuffs without space and facilities for storage,
along with the prolonged delay of command to sell, has led
to a total waste in many instances. Despite a nationwide drive
for modernization of agriculture by means of modern
Czechoslovakian tractors and chemical fertilizers and insecti-
cides, neither productivity nor the effort to increase it seem
to improve in the rural economy of Burma. The loss of about
100 state machine tractor stations, for example, brought a
resulting loss of from K. 2. 2 million in 1962-63 to K. 17. 677
million in 1964-65, [47] forcing the government to attempt to
auction off over 4, 000 tractors in 1967-68, with no buyers in
sight. In brief, the objective of increasing purchasing power
and production in the socialist economy of Burma today remains an ideal rather than a reality. Indeed, the thesis of
"planned chaos" advanced by Ludwig von Mises seems to apply
rigorously to the experiment of a command economy by the
Revolutionary Council Government. [48]

The macroeconomic indicators of Burma's stagnation
presented before may not do justice to the ultimate cause of
the Burmese Way to Socialism. As pointed out earlier, the
economic objectives of the Revolutionary Council Government
gave priority to equity rather than efficiency in adopting the
model of a command economy. Perhaps some equity has been
achieved in the total nationalization of the economy; and the
political necessity of catering to the peasants through massive
economic and technical aid may have transferred some of the
income of the wealthy to the poor. Even at that, it is still uncertain as to how much of the national wealth, along with
social and economic privileges, has accrued to the ruling

military elite and the black marketeers, whose access to
nationalized goods and services has been rather complete
under the Burmese Way to Socialism. In view of the drastic
decline in output and a surprising increase in the rate of population in the 1960s, the benevolent objectives of equity and
justice seem to be obliterated. Indeed, equity in a world of
national poverty has very little meaning in the process of
modernization.

Neither the factor endowment nor the social institution
of Burma seems to fit the requisite pattern of revolutionary
socialism. For one thing, not until recently has Burma ever
suffered from the kind of abject poverty that has historically
plagued countries like India and China; thus, the poverty
thesis of revolutionary socialism does not apply. For another
there has never been a class of landed bourgeois or an op-
pressed proletariat in the traditional social system that can
be compared to the feudalism of early Western Europe. Particularly important is the fact that whatever alien system of
landlordism had existed in colonial Burma, it was ended by
the time of independence, when land and other natural resources were nationalized by the Burmese Government.

Having no serious problems of abject poverty, Malthusian
population pressure and glaring inequity in income distribution
the choice of revolutionary socialism by the present military
government and of evolutionary socialism by the previous
civilian government has been Burma's Pandora's box. The
main reasons for this choice, apparently, lie not in the histor
ical materialism of Marxism but in the traditional value syste
and historical experiences of Burma, which have augmented
the inward-looking character of the Burmese personality and
social system. [49]

The asceticism of Buddhism might not have prevented the
Burmese from enjoying the material welfare, as W. A. Lewis
has argued, [50] or from engaging in profit-making black marke
activities; yet, it provides some congeniality to the illusive
theses of "a pernicious economic system," exploitation of the
greedy bourgeois and "immiserization" of the masses. From
the concept of life as a whirlpool of sufferings to the philosoph
of becoming as reflected in the concept of impermanency,
certain values and outlooks of Buddhism may be taken as som
what similar to the dialectics of Marx. Without delving too
far into the philosophical affinity between Burmese Buddhism
and Marxism (which, incidentally, has not been resolved in
the modern political philosophy of Burma), I shall argue that
this illusive affinity, strengthened by the traditional nationalis

and traumatic experiences under colonial rule, has been the
main cause of adopting socialism in Burma. Under military
rule, nationalism tends to be more aggressive and militant;
and revolutionary socialism seems to fit the personality of
the military elite, as well as the power structure of the military polity, in Burma. It will also be argued that the very
traditional value system and experiences that led to the choice
of revolutionary socialism are responsible for the failures in
the construction of a command economy in Burma.

The basic tendencies of Buddhism in Burma--to desocialize
the individual, to develop a fatalistic attitude toward life and
one's station and to encourage spending rather than saving*--
all seem to be incompatible with the materialism and divinity
of work embodied in the philosophy of Marxian socialism.
This is not to say that Burmese Buddhism contains no dynamic
elements for modernization via socialism, but rather that the
appeal of modern socialist ideals to the Burmese political
leadership has been in the realm of emotions rather than
actions. Paradoxically, the unsuccessful tuning of the basic
antimaterialistic tenets of Buddhism to the historical materialism of Marx has produced the surprising result of stimulating
capitalistic endeavor for the masses. A century of experiencing
individualism under colonial capitalism, with whatever freedom of choice the Burmese were exposed to under British and
civilian governments, has been the upsetting factor in the
Burmese Way to Socialism. Perhaps, the propounders of the
Burmese Way to Socialism are correct in their diagnosis that
the Burmese have been infatuated with the mentality of the
bourgeois. [51] Whatever the case, the value-orientation of the
Burmese actors, including the military elite, is more individualistic than collectivistic, more disorganizational than
organizational, and more acquisitive than ascetic with respect
to spending, in terms of both traditional value systems and
historical experience.

These factors, plus the relatively egalitarian social
structure of traditional Burmese society, with its affluence
in basic necessities, may be taken as major determinants of
the economic chaos that occurred under military management.

---

*The improvident character of the Burmese culture is
not generally agreed upon among social scientists. Lucien
Pye and E. E. Hagen theoretically advanced and confirmed
it, while Manning Nash observed otherwise; see Manning Nash,
The Golden Road to Modernity: Village Life in Contemporary
Burma (New York: J. Wiley & Sons, 1965), pp. 156-65.

In short, the requirements for building a command economy
of proportional development, which the Revolutionary Council
Government undertook, are greater, both economically and
culturally, than those of an evolutionary socialism adopted by
the former civilian government. Indeed, in retrospect, the
limited economic achievements of the Pyidawtha Government
(U Nu Government) in the 1950s look gigantic, compared with
those of the present military government.

Demonetization and Its Repercussions

At the very outset, it must be remembered that nationalization of banks and demonetization of K. 100 and K. 50 notes
were formally aimed at achieving equity in income distribution
and penalizing the obstructors of the socialist economy. They
were sequential measures of direct war waged against the
opposition to the construction of the socialist economy. The
opposition was, of course, supposed to have been given by
the domestic and foreign capitalists, who were held responsible for manipulating prices and exploiting the masses with
their stock of money.

Actually, the demonetization measure was undertaken
to correct the inefficiency and uncontrollable repercussions
of the nationalization of banks, along with trade and industry.
Inefficiency in the nationalization of banks was reflected in
news leakages and failures in planning, supervision and implementation, which led to a massive evasion and withdrawal
of funds from the banks in 1963. The same defects in the
total nationalization of the economy and the introduction of an
inappropriate rationing system created a nationwide black
market, with hyperinflation of a kind unique to the command
economy of Burma.

By imposing a capital levy on the surrendered notes, the
demonetization measure was a de facto antiinflationary device
for reducing the quantity of money in circulation. The contrived scarcity created by the economic policy of rationing,
the massive withdrawal of funds, and liberal credit programs
for the peasants seem to have produced a classic inflation in
terms of the quantity theory of money.

Theoretically, demonetization of K. 100 and K. 50 notes
may be taken as a direct application of the quantity theory of
money--to deflate the general price level by reducing the total
value of money in the hands of the people and of capitalists,
in particular. With respect to that and to various economic
repercussions of nationalization of banks and businesses, the

Revolutionary Council explained the raison d'être for demonetization measure as follows:

> Since the Burmese Way to Socialism does not serve
> the interest of the exploiters and profiteers these
> domestic and foreign capitalists began to withdraw
> their deposits from the banks to oppose the national-
> ization of banks. When foreign trade was nationalized
> in order to prevent the incommensurate rise in the
> prices of consumer goods for the working people or
> when the wholesale houses, big stores and brokerage
> houses were nationalized, they began to liquidate
> and from the withdrawal of deposits they began to
> speculate in commodities so as to obtain quick and
> large profits. [52]

Further, it asserted that these speculators or profiteers
used their funds as exchange commodities to play havoc with
the national economy. The volume of K. 100 and K. 50 notes
was supposed to increase rapidly in the hands of these capitalists, and the government was thus forced to demonetize them
to counteract the economic havoc of inflation and exploitation. [53]
    Even if all these observations are true, one has to admit
that the basic fault lies in the ineffectual method of nationalization employed by the government. The immense complexity
of enforcing laws and checking the inevitable multiple evasion
attending a system of direct controls are also apparent in
these observations. In addition, the process of liquidation of
assets by the capitalists (referred to in the above statement)
seems to negate the very premise upon which the basic argument for building a command economy was made by the Revolutionary Council, i.e., the concentration of income and wealth
in the hands of the capitalists and landlords. It is curious as
to where and how the transfer of titles of assets was made,
in view of the fact that, historically, the liquidators were the
possessors of all wealth and exploiters of the masses in
Burma. Granting that such a liquidation took place, it would
seem that the distribution of wealth had not altered significantly
to improve the lot of the working people, since the transfer
of titles to assets must lie elsewhere in the economy of Burma.
    At this juncture, the major aspects of economic analysis
given by the propounders of the Burmese Way to Socialism on
the objectives and effects of demonetization deserve attention.
On the evening of May 17, 1964, the Revolutionary Council
promulgated its Law No. 7, by which all K. 100 notes and K. 50

notes were declared unusable as legal tender. It improvised
further that these notes must be surrendered to the governmen
no later than May 24, with an initial promise of redeeming
on the spot the notes up to the value of K. 500.

Actual redemption of that value lasted only a day--May
18--and, on the following day, the redemption amount was
reduced to K. 200 only. On May 20, the redemption was completely stopped. [54] The main reason for this was, obviously,
a massive surrender of notes and the government's inability
to determine the sources of funds.

The four specific aims and provisions of the Demonetization Law were given as follows:

1. The primary target of demonetization is the
    indigenous and foreign capitalists who have
    for many years unfairly accumulated the
    people's money with which they now oppose
    the Burmese Way to Socialism. The major
    aim is to destroy the monetary weapon of
    these capitalists who have hindered the
    growth in the well-being of peasants, skilled
    and unskilled labor or the working people
    as a whole.
2. In order to avoid harming the innocent or
    honest savers and the poor, the value of
    surrendered notes up to K. 4, 200 will be
    completely redeemed.
3. On the basis of humanitarian considerations,
    the same amount of redemption will be made
    according to size even to the savers of large
    sums of money through dishonest means.
4. With the aim of national unity, those who
    committed the crimes in connection with
    these illegal tenders will be granted either
    a complete amnesty or light sentences. [55]

The entire argument for demonetization seems to hinge,
therefore, upon the single premise that most of the notes of
larger denomination were in the hands of the indigenous and
foreign capitalists, who were held solely responsible for op-
posing the Burmese Way to Socialism by using these notes.
Implicit in the above statements is the indeterminateness of
the government's approach, on the one hand, and the inability
to detect the sources of notes, on the other. To begin with,
the period of surrender as well as the rates of redemption are

too liberal for an effective demonetization. [56] The second and
third provisions of the Law might have been a benevolent ges-
ture of the government in accordance with the Burmese Way
to Socialism; yet, they certainly became major avenues for
evading demonetization, as statistical data provided by the
Revolutionary Council itself proves. As to the last provision,
there can be little doubt about the inability to determine the
sources of notes, even though the government required filing
of application for the surrender of notes after May 20 and up
to May 24. The statistics on the value of notes in circulation
and the surrendered amounts are given in Table 5.

The value of surrendered notes was roughly 78 percent
of the total value of K. 100 and K. 50 notes in circulation,
leaving about 22 percent illegal tenders in the hands of the
people. Since the value of surrendered notes up to K. 4, 200
was completely redeemed, the total amount of demonetized
notes would be much less than K. 930 million in terms of rein-
jecting the money into circulation. This simple swap between
K. 100 and K. 50 notes and other notes of lesser denomination
was a dampening factor in reducing the quantity of money as
well as the extent of demonetization. Moreover, the value of
surrendered notes above K. 4, 200 was not completely demonetized, since the government applied only a graduated income
tax rate on it, thereby reducing the extent of demonetization.
In a sense, demonetization of this kind was tantamount to a
tax on cash assets outside banks. According to the Budget
Report of the Revolutionary Council to the People (1964-65),
the total amount of redemption was given as K. 650 million,
or the total tax collected by the government from those whose
value of surrendered notes exceeded the K. 4, 200 tax-exempted
limit and which also happened to be a tax-exempted income
since 1954. [57] If one assumes that the unsurrendered notes
were no longer used as money by the people, the total value
of demonetized notes would be roughly K. 552 million, or
about 46 percent of the total value of K. 100 and K. 50 notes
in circulation on May 17. The same Report gave an estimate
of the "total currency notes circulating in the hands of the
people" on October 1, 1964, as K. 2. 150 billion, K. 1. 50 billion
plus K. 650 million redeemed by the government. * It is,

---

*If one takes this literally to mean notes in the hands of
the nonbanking public, the concept of quantity of money employed by the Revolutionary Council is, indeed, revolutionary.
I suspect, however, that this is the case, since the quantity
seems to be far too exaggerated. For example, The Quarterly

TABLE 5

Value of Notes in Circulation and Surrendered
Notes, Burma, May, 1964

Number	Items	Kyats
1	Value of K. 100 and K. 50 Notes in Circulation on May 17, 1964	1, 202, 167, 050
2	Value of K. 100 and K. 50 Notes Surrendered to the Government	930, 777, 300
3=(1-2)	Value of Unsurrendered Notes	271, 389, 750

Source: Central Organization Committee, BSPP, The
Economic Affairs of the Burma Socialist Program Party No.
1 (In Burmese) (Rangoon: Sarpai Beitman Press, 1965), p.
45.

therefore, logical to assume that this amount was totally made
up of notes with less than K. 50 denomination. From this data,
the total value of currency notes in circulation at the time of
demonetization may be estimated at K. 2. 70 billion. The actua
decline of currency notes in circulation due to demonetization,
therefore, was about 20 percent, or K. 552 million out of
K. 2. 7 billion. [58] However, the exclusion of demand deposits
from the quantity of money is illegitimate.

From all available data other than the above Report, it
seems that the quantity of money--defined properly as currency in circulation plus demand deposits in the People's Bank
of Burma--did not decline at all, contrary to what the Revolutionary Council claimed, between 1964 and 1965. The figures
for currency in circulation in 1964 and 1965 were given by The
Quarterly Bulletin of Statistics as K. 1. 887253 billion and
K. 1. 765620 billion, while demand deposits in the People's
Banks for the same years were given as K. 749. 635 million
and K. 903. 280 million, respectively. [59] Between 1964 and

Bulletin of Statistics: Fourth Quarter 1966 (in English) gave
the total value of currency in circulation for 1964 as K. 1. 8872
billion. See Bulletin of Statistics: Fourth Quarter 1966
(Rangoon: Central Press, Central Statistics and Economic
Department, 1966), p. 124.

1965, therefore, the quantity of money remained virtually
unchanged at about K. 2. 6 billion. The only significant change
was in the composition of the stock of money, particularly
the fact that, by 1965, all notes in circulation were less than
K. 50 in denomination. This, plus an additional issue of about
14 million coins, in relation to the shortage of goods and
services, may be taken as evidence that there was a sharp
increase in the average velocity of transactions in Burma, to
explain the phenomenal increase of prices in the private black
market. This change in the velocity of circulation can also
be explained by monetary insecurity, or a lack of confidence
in the national currency, within the total climate of nationalization and demonetization. This ineffectiveness of demonetization as an antiinflationary device in Burma by no means in-
validates the quantity theory of money, though its basic
assumption of a stable velocity of circulation is at stake.

Since a basic objective of demonetization is to combat
the countervailing monetary power of the capitalists, its effectiveness in subduing them may be examined in the light of
statistics provided by the Revolutionary Council Government.
In a statistical table of thirty-three different values of surrendered notes, number of surrenderers as between aliens
and natives, the range of total value of notes, [60] and the nature
of income distribution prior to demonetization was explained
at length by using a comparative analysis of the number of
people who had surrendered the notes and the working population.

In this connection, the analyst of demonetization made an
interesting but wrong, observation: since the working population in 1964 numbered 8 million and the number of people who
had surrendered the notes was only 1, 364, 002, it meant that
83 percent of the working population was so poor that they
could not even use K. 50 notes. The basic fallacy of such a
socialist-biased observation lies in the analyst's inability to
comprehend the basic nature of money and its use. In the
words of A. G. Hart, ". . . to use money in a transaction
does not use it up, "[61] and to compute the poverty of the masses
in terms of the number of surrenderers is to commit the
logical fallacy of petitio principii. For all we know, the
working people might have wound up with all the K. 100 and
K. 50 notes that the capitalists liquidated into other assets and
commodities, as was initially claimed by the Revolutionary
Council. [62] In an attempt to explain the skewness of the distribution of people surrendering notes at the levels of K. 200
and K. 500, the Revolutionary Council charged that the

capitalists were guilty of using agents for the redemption of
these notes. It is equally feasible to assume that the surrenderers of notes below K. 4, 200 were mostly ordinary working people in the middle income bracket. On the whole, the
number of people who surrendered the notes above the value
of K. 4, 200 constituted less than 2 percent of the total population of surrenderers. [63] From this, one may assert that there
were very few capitalists or rich people in the country with
a taxable income of over K. 4, 200. To determine the level of
income or richness of persons on the basis of different values
of notes surrendered to the government makes no more sense
than to say that those who did not surrender the notes were
poor. In short, the statistics on the distribution of people
according to the various values of surrendered notes is a poor
guideline for determining the pattern of income distribution.

What is most significant is the evasion of demonetization
and a capital levy on cash assets by a relatively wealthy class
of people, which the Revolutionary Council itself admitted.
To counter those who might argue that the study of statistics
on the surrender of notes is insufficient to determine who owns
K. 100 and K. 50 notes on the ground that people, in general,
use both cash and demand deposits as money, the Revolutionar
Council explicitly stated that the poor did not use checking
accounts, which is quite valid in Burma. (It should also be
noted that most Burmese, including the urbanites and the rich,
use cash.) It went on to state further that just prior to the
announcement of demonetization, the capitalists, who primaril
used checking accounts, withdrew funds in K. 100 and K. 50
notes from banks. Indeed, it is quite incredible that these
clever and exploiting profit-mongers would venture to assume
such a risk with a full knowledge of pending demonetization.
Most likely, they would have withdrawn their funds in notes of
smaller denomination and liquidated whatever K. 100 and K. 50
notes they happened to own. Even if the record of 7, 550 persons either withdrawing funds or closing accounts at banks
between August, 1963, and December, 1963[64] is true, the
time period of four months before the demonetization date of
May 17, 1964, would have been long enough to evade the goverr
ment measure. If anything, the primary fault of letting these
so-called capitalists "play havoc with the economy and the
standard of living of the working people" lies in the deficient
method of demonetization employed by the government.

In order to justify further the Burmese Way to Socialism
and the demonetization measure, a statistical table of income
taxpayers for the three periods 1939-40, 1947-48 and 1961-62[6]

was drawn up, with the single purpose of proving the growth
of capitalists and of inequity in income distribution under the
civilian government. The unfortunate result of this, in my
opinion, is to show a relatively prosperous economy of rising
income and an upward climbing of lower income groups in the
distribution of income. As for the nature of income distribution, the number of taxpayers and the changes among various
taxable income brackets should not, and could not, provide a
satisfactory answer. For one thing, farmers in Burma have
been exempted from the personal income tax throughout the
period of independence. [*] All that the statistical table indicates
is the distribution of taxpayers, not of tax burdens, among
various taxable income brackets. Moreover, the income taxpayers, or wage earners, in government services, business
and industry, along with a few private businesses, accounted
for less than 25 percent of the working population. The table
also shows a rise in the number of taxpayers within the first
taxable income bracket (K. 1,000 to K.2,000) of from 76 to
628 between 1948 and 1968. [66] It would be appropriate to consider this as an indicator of vertical mobility among relatively
poor persons or families in the distribution of income. Furthermore, the levels of taxable income with the largest concentration
of taxpayers were the middle income brackets of K. 3,501 to
K. 5,000, K. 5,001 to K. 7,500 and K. 7,501 to K. 10,000 in both
1948 and 1962, indicating a normal distribution of taxpayers. [67]
In the absence of dependable statistical data on the percentage
distribution of individuals and families among various levels
of income in the Burmese economy, the relative shares of
national output or equity in income distribution cannot be determined. Without dwelling too much on the unreliability and
shortage of statistical data in an underdeveloped economy such
as Burma, it can be bluntly stated that the proof provided by
the Revolutionary Council of glaring inequity in the distribution
of Burmese income under civilian government is a myth.

Another note of interest, put forth on the basis of the
same statistical data, was an increase in the number of taxpayers by about four times between 1948 and 1968, which was
interpreted as the rise of the bourgeois under the perverted

---

[*]This has accounted for the small tax base for personal
income tax in independent Burma, a sound point emphasized
by Richard A. Musgrave in his advice on tax reforms to the
Pyidawtha Government; see, L. J. Walinsky, Economic Development of Burma (1951-60) (New York: The Twentieth Century
Fund, 1962), chap. 25.

socialism of the Pyidawtha Government. Even more curious
was an observation, made in the same vein of socialist stigma,
on the evidence of tax evasion by rich capitalists. Evidence
was given, based on a comparison between the number of taxpayers in 1961-62 and the number of surrenderers of K. 100
and K. 50 notes in 1964. Using the fact that the latter were
more numerous than the former as an indicator of tax evasion,
it was concluded that the capitalists had not only exploited the
masses but, also, had cheated the government. This conclusion was drawn from two value-loaded premises: (a) the
surrenderers of K. 100 and K. 50 notes, in general, were rich
taxpayers with a personal income in excess of K. 4, 200, a
formidable definition of capitalists under the Burmese Way
to Socialism and (b) the surrendering of these notes was an
unmistakable indicator of capitalists' accumulated savings,
or a high propensity to save. [68]
    On the face of it, these premises and inferences are more
of an emotional exercise than an intellectual one. To equate
income taxpayers and surrenderers of the notes with tax-
evading capitalists and propensity to surrender the notes with
that of a high propensity to save through tax evasion and so
forth is merely begging the question and saying whatever one
wishes to say. What seems most contradictory, however, is
that if these premises and inferences were truly embraced by
the Revolutionary Council as the sacred tenets of the Burmese
Way to Socialism, why did they initially admit, in passing the
Demonetization Law, the possibility that there might be honest
savers among the surrenderers of notes valued under K. 4, 200?
Or why did the Revolutionary Council allow a double exemption
of ordinary income tax and the capital levy for those dishonest
savers? The answers to these questions are to be found not
in the so-called humanitarian considerations of the Revolutionary Council but in the lack of know-how, apparatus and resources to enforce and control the Demonetization Law and,
most important of all, the social and political necessity of
not harming the relatively well-off class of military political
elite and sympathizers of the BSPP.
    Last, but not the least interesting, the Revolutionary
Council concluded that there were many foreign capitalists
operating and exploiting the masses in the Burmese economy
prior to 1962. The proof of this, once again, was given by
comparing the relative ratios of aliens to the total population
of Burma and to the population of surrenderers of notes. Since
the percentage of aliens with respect to the total surrenderers was 6. 37, and the aliens constituted only 2. 08 percent of

the total population of Burma in 1964, the Burmese economy
under civilian government was inferred to have been dominated
by alien capitalists. [69] This conclusion was supplemented by
a more specific comparison of the relative ratios of aliens to
natives in the three levels of value of the surrendered notes--
such as one alien out of every twenty-nine natives at the level
of K. 100, one alien out of every thirty-one natives at the level
of above K. 1, 000 and one alien out of every nine natives at the
level of above K. 100, 000. [70] Without explaining the decline in
percentage of aliens between the first and the second levels,
the Council generalized that a sudden jump in percentage in
the last level meant the usurpation of economic opportunities
by alien capitalists in the Burmese economy. I suspect, however, that despite the distinct possibility of aliens--mostly
Chinese and Indians--being relatively richer than Burmese
on the average, the above ratios might have been due to factors
other than the ones emphasized by the Revolutionary Council.
They might be due to differences in cultural habits and economic
behavior--parsimony, for instance--between the aliens and
Burmese, or to the lesser ability of aliens to evade by using
native agents in a political climate of outright discrimination
against aliens. Perhaps, the greatest burden of the capital
levy on surrendered notes was borne by alien capitalists, or
the largest benefit from evasion of demonetization had accrued
to the so-called domestic capitalists. In a command economy
of planned chaos, with a poor record of economic activities
and status of various social groups, quantitative proofs of
economic perversion are virtually impossible. It may be ascertained, however, that the demonetization measure of the
Revolutionary Council has accomplished very little with respect to its basic goals, except for the psychic income derived
from the assertion of supernationalism, socialism and anti-
alienism.

NOTES

1. Cf. P. N. Rosenstein-Rodan, "The Role of Income
Distribution in Development Programs, " reprint from essay
written for volume in honor of Marco Fanno by Massachusetts
Institute of Technology Center for International Studies, Rivista
Internazionale di Scienze Economiche Commerciali (Milan:
May, 1965).

148   BURMA AND PAKISTAN

2. Myron Weiner, ed., Modernization (New York:
Basic Books, Inc., 1966).

3. Max F. Millikan, Criteria for Decision Making in
Economic Planning (Cambridge, Mass.: Center for International Studies, 1962), p. 1.

4. See Rosenstein-Rodan, op. cit., p. 1.

5. W. M. Dobell, "Ayub Khan as President of Pakistan,"
Pacific Affairs, XLII, 3 (Fall, 1969), 308.

6. See E. E. Hagen, "Power Structure and Economic
Development," Asia, 16 (New York: The Asia Society, Autumn
1969), p. 6.

7. See R. V. Weeks, Pakistan: Birth and Growth of a
Muslim Nation (Princeton, N. J.: D. Van Nostrand Co.,
1964), p. 167.

8. Swadesh R. Bose, "Trend of Real Income of the Rural
Poor in East Pakistan 1947-1966," Pakistan Development Review, VIII, 3 (Autumn, 1968), 457.

9. See Arthur MacEwan, "Problems of Interregional and
Intersectoral Allocation: The Case of Pakistan," Pakistan
Development Review, X, 1 (Spring, 1970), 11.

10. Sayed N. H. Naqvi, "Some Comments on Planning
Experience in Pakistan," Pakistan Development Review
(Autumn, 1968), p. 406.

11. Ibid.

12. See Azizur R. Khan, "Some Notes on Planning Experience in Pakistan," Pakistan Development Review (Autumn,
1968), pp. 425-27; also, Gustav Papanek, Pakistan's Development: Social Goals and Private Incentives (Cambridge, Mass.
Harvard University Press, 1967), pp. 199-200.

13. R. H. Khander, "Concentration of Economic Power
in Pakistan," A. M. Ghouse, ed., Studies in Economic Development: With Special Reference to Pakistan (Lahore: The
Businessmen Seminar, 1962), p. 170.

14. See Mahbubul Haq, Speech at the Second Management Convention in Karachi, quoted in The Business Recorder (Karachi), April, 25, 1968.

15. See Papanek, op. cit., p. 149; also, Sayed M. Hussain, "The Effect of Growing Constraint of Subsistence Farming on Farmer Response to Price: A Case Study of Jute in Pakistan, " Pakistan Development Review, IX, 3 (Autumn, 1969). Hussain observed that, in East Pakistan, constraints, such as subsistence farming and lack of credit, may grow in time, thereby limiting farmer response to price.

16. A. H. M. N. Chowdhury, "Some Reflections on Income Redistributive Intermediation in Pakistan, " Pakistan Development Review, IX, 2 (Summer, 1969), 109.

17. For counterarguments to Papanek's see S. R. Bose, "Pakistan's Development--The Role of Government and Private Enterprise, " Pakistan Development Review, VIII, 2 (Summer, 1968).

18. Cf. Henry Smith, The Economics of Socialism Reconsidered (London: Oxford University Press, 1962), p. 95.

19. See Laura Randall, ed., Economic Development: Evolution or Revolution (Boston: D. C. Heath & Co., 1964), p. viii.

20. Party Seminar 1965 . . ., (Rangoon: Sarpay Beikman Press, BSPP, February, 1966), pp. 100-101.

21. Ibid., p. 101.

22. Address delivered by General Ne Win, Fourth Party Seminar, Nov. 6th, 1969 (Rangoon: Central Press, BSPP, 1969), p. 24.

23. Party Seminar, 1965 . . ., p. 28.

24. The Philosophy of the Burma Socialist Programme Party: The System of Correlation of Man and His Environment (Rangoon: Ministry of Information, 1963), p. 45.

25. Party Seminar 1965 . . ., p. 33.

26. Aung Than Tun, Four Eras of Burmese Law (in Burmese) (Rangoon: Sanbe Press, 1968), pp. 219-20.

27. Party Seminar, 1965 . . ., p. 64.

28. For details, see Aung Than Tun, op. cit., pp. 224-26

29. See A. C. Pigou, Socialism versus Capitalism (London: Macmillan & Co., 1960), pp. 6-11.

30. See Party Seminar 1965 . . ., p. 95.

31. See Robert Keatley, "Burma's Sticky 'Way to Socialism,' " The Wall Street Journal (New York), September, 16, 1968, p. 16.

32. Party Seminar, 1965 . . ., p. 78.

33. Ibid., p. 79.

34. Ibid.

35. From my survey on agricultural cooperation in Burma during 1961-62.

36. "The Newsletter on Party's Affairs No. 5, 1964" (In Burmese) (Rangoon: The Central Organizing Committee, 1964), p. 17.

37. The Working People's Daily (Rangoon), March 17, 1969, p. 3.

38. "The Newsletter on Party's Affairs No. 3, Special Issue on Peasants' Day" (In Burmese) (Rangoon: Central Organizing Committee, BSPP, 1966), p. 12. (Hereafter cited as "Newsletter, No. 3, 1966.")

39. Party Seminar 1965 . . ., p. 80; also, Mya Maung, "Agricultural Cooperation in Burma: A Study on the Value-Orientation and Effects of Socio-Economic Action," Social and Economic Studies, XIV, 4 (Jamaica: University of the West Indies, December, 1965), 330-31.

40. "Newsletter, No. 3, 1966," pp. 7 and 14.

41. See J. V. Levin, The Export Economies: Their
Pattern of Development in Historical Perspective (Cambridge,
Mass.: Harvard University Press, 1960), pp. 241-48; also
Hla Myint, The Economics of the Developing Countries (New
York: Frederick A. Praeger, Inc., 1964), p. 52.

42. "The Newsletter on Party's Affairs No. 1, 1966"
(Rangoon: Central Organizing Committee, 1966), p. 10.

43. Ibid.

44. Ibid. and L. J. Walinsky, Economic Development of
Burma (1951-60) (New York: The Twentieth Century Fund,
1962), p. 292.

45. Sources for this are Burmese refugees and speeches
of General Ne Win at party seminar, 1965.

46. See J. E. Meade, The Stationery Economy (London:
G. Allen and Unwin, 1965), p. 15.

47. Report of the Revolutionary Council to the People on
the Budget Estimates of the Revolutionary Council Government
of the Union of Burma for 1965-66 (Rangoon: Central Press,
1965), p. 8.

48. See Ludwig von Mises, Planned Chaos (New York:
The Foundation for Economic Education, 1947), pp. 32-34.

49. Professor E. E. Hagen termed these "retreatism"
and "status withdrawal" in the doubly plural society of colonial
Burma; see his The Theory of Social Change (Homewood, Ill.:
The Dorsey Press, 1963), chap. 11.

50. See W. A. Lewis, The Theory of Economic Growth
(Homewood: R. D. Irwin, Inc., 1955), pp. 24-25.

51. See Party Seminar 1965 . . ., p. 101.

52. Party Seminar 1965 . . ., pp. 93-94.

53. Ibid., p. 94.

54. See Central Organization Committee, BSPP, The Economic Affairs of the Burma Socialist Program Party No. 1 (In Burmese) (Rangoon: Sarpai Beitman Press, 1965), p. 54. (Hereafter cited as The Economic Affairs of the BSPP No. 1 . . . .)

55. Ibid., pp. 65-66.

56. A point emphasized by Professor G. N. Halm of the Fletcher School of Law and Diplomacy, Tufts University.

57. "The Newsletter on Party's Affairs No. 3, 1964" (In Burmese) (Rangoon: The Central Organizing Committee, October, 1964), p. 29. (Hereafter cited as "Newsletter, No. 3, 1964 . . . ."

58. "Newsletter, No. 3, 1964 . . .," p. 29.

59. Quarterly Bulletin of Statistics, op. cit., p. 122.

60. The Economic Affairs of the BSPP No. 1 . . ., pp. 43-44.

61. A. G. Hart, Money, Debt and Economic Activity (2d ed.; New York: Prentice-Hall, 1953), p. 155.

62. See Party Seminar 1965 . . ., p. 94.

63. The Economic Affairs of the BSPP No. 1 . . ., p. 58.

64. Ibid., p. 56.

65. Ibid., p. 60.

66. The Economic Affairs of the BSPP, No. 1 . . ., p. 58

67. Ibid.

68. Ibid., pp. 62-64.

69. Ibid., p. 48.

70. Ibid., pp. 49-50.

CHAPTER **6** CONCLUSIONS

From the foregoing analysis of development experiences in Burma and Pakistan, two general conclusions may be derived: (a) the economic actions and policies of development pursued by the LDCs are an integral part of the complex processes of social conflict and (b) relative achievements or failures in development attempts are a direct function of the relative degree of societal openness. The receptivity of a social system to the inflow of advanced technology and capital is governed by the historical social conflict within and without a particular society, on the one hand, and by the nature of its social and political structure, on the other. As the cases of Burma and Pakistan testify, most traditional societies in their historic transformation tend to insulate themselves in the face of certain threats to traditional institutions. The degree of societal insulation from the currents of modernity differ from country to country, depending upon the types of social conflict, type of social transfusion of modern value systems, cultural homogeneity and the basic economic security of a social system. Economic change, whether outergenerated or innergenerated, is not a simple matter of importing and imitating advanced socioeconomic systems and methods of organization, but also of effective transformation of wants, motivations and values within a traditional society. One of the most difficult obstacles to modernization lies in the rigidity of the value systems, which, irrationally, resist the inevitable sacrifice of certain traditional institutions.

The overall willingness of the Pakistani political elite to pay a cultural price, in contrast to Burma's obsession with traditional cultural integrity, has led to the adoption of certain types of development policies and goals. In Burma, the historical social conflict and the interplay of religion, philosophy and politics have tended to encourage inward-looking policies. The paradoxical development of Pakistan in "confounding the prophets," on the other hand, has been due--in the light of Weberian thesis--more to the receptivity of its social system to change than to the simple dismantling of state controls as

153

such. The Pakistani value system, as manifested in the
attitudes and motivations of the ruling social and political
elites, seems to have undergone a kind of Protestant Reformation earlier than Burma. It is this precedence in cultural
change that accounts for a greater degree of societal openness
in Pakistan, as well as its achievement in development.

The most paradoxical and interesting contrast in development policies, measures and goals is that socioeconomic
structures seem to call for the exact opposite of the economic
models used in the actual experiment. In Pakistan, an apparent socioeconomic rigidity in terms of mobility and inequity
in income distribution seems to demand a revolutionary approach, whereas the relatively egalitarian socioeconomic
structure of Burma seems to call for an evolutionary approach.
Yet, the opposite pattern of development has emerged in the
two countries.

The reason for this divergence lies in the realm of the
ideals, motivations, emotions and personalities of the political
elite that came to dominate the polity, as well as in the sociopolitical conditions after independence. The historical continuum of the role of a Western-trained and Western-oriented
social group in the Pakistani polity and the decline of such a
group in Burma are major determinants of each country's
development policy and goals. Such a simple explanation, however, must be supplemented by an understanding of the nature
of traditional social and value systems and of the social conflic
and changes that took place during and after colonial rule. Onl
the historical intragroup tension and conflict within Burma and
Pakistan, therefore, can explain the paradoxical development
of ideologies that do not seem to fit either the religious philosophy or actual socioeconomic structure of the two countries.

Part of the appeal of modern capitalism to Pakistan, or
the appeal of socialism to Burma, may be explained in terms
of their respective traditional value systems as fostered by
religion. Comparative analysis of the religious philosophy of
the two countries seems to contradict the compatibility of
capitalist ideology with Islamic social structure or the compatibility of socialist ideology with Buddhist social structure.
Religion cannot be taken as a static parameter in explaining
the raison d'être of ideological commitment to certain "isms."
Certain religious concepts--such as impermanency and suffering in Burma's Buddhist philosophy--found their profound
expression in the adoption of Marxist ideologies. In Pakistan,
an ancient Islamic philosophy came to incorporate modern
values in the hands of Mohammad Iqbal and other lay

philosophers, long before independence. This has not been
true in Burma, where religious philosophy remains the sole
property of the clerical order. To date, no significant reformation or attempt to reconcile modern values with those of
religion has been made in Burma, and the resulting ideological
crisis--the diffusion of Marxism in a Buddhist country--is
Burma's most critical problem, which neither the civilian
government nor the present Revolutionary Council Government has yet been able to resolve. Socialism as a means of
reviving traditional institutions has not been effective in Burma,
due, basically, to certain fundamental cleavages between
traditional value systems and the Marxist prescription for
sociopolitical and economic revolution. In actuality, Pakistan's
development policy has been more revolutionary than that of
Burma in respect to social change.

An important factor contributing to the adoption of different
developmental ideologies in Burma and Pakistan is related to
international social conflict. Indo-Pakistani rivalry before and
after partition has its counterpart in the choice by Pakistan of
a development policy different from its neighbor. The fear of
alien influence--particularly the West--the continual presence
and dominance of the Indian and Chinese entrepreneurs, and
the impact of the Cold War in Southeast Asia have led Burma
to follow socialism and massive state controls. Although
physical insulation of the social system from alien encroachment is possible for Burma through its command economy,
ideological neutrality is a myth as far as the formulation and
dissemination of the Burmese Way to Socialism is concerned.
Burmese socialism contains more alien doctrines from the
Sino-Soviet world than it does from Burmese philosophy.

Economic policy and its implementation in Burma and
Pakistan may be taken as a special case study of experiments
with two models of economic organization and growth: the
revolutionary versus the evolutionary approach to development,
or a command economy of total state control and enterprise
versus a modern welfare state with heavy emphasis on private
enterprise. As to the priority of economic goals, development
strategy and planning in the two countries indicate a contrast
in equity versus productivity. The case of Pakistan seems to
follow the strategy of letting the size of the economic cake
grow first and of sharing it equally later, while the opposite
holds true for Burma. Social and economic repercussions
testify that the two goals are not simultaneously attainable and
that the relative neglect of either one has serious economic
and political consequences. The effect of too much preoccupation

with efficiency or productivity in the development programming
of Pakistan has been to widen the gap between urban and rural
standards of living, the rich minority and the poor majority,
as well as the economic growth of West and East wings. The
intragroup and regional disparities in wealth and living standar
were the major source of political crisis and unrest in the late
1960s in Pakistan, whereas Burma's excessive preoccupation
with distributive equity and an ideal socialist economy has resulted in an economic disaster of inefficiency and stagnation.

The lesson to be learned from development in Pakistan
confirms the theory that price systems and market mechanism
can be useful devices for stimulating private incentive and
enterprise. Despite some inequity in income distribution, the
economic performance of Pakistan under the liberalizing regir
of the Ayub Khan Government has been remarkable in reaching
a stage of self-sufficiency in agriculture and a compounded
rate of industrial growth. Though this performance cannot be
attributed, simply, to the age-old issue of state versus private
enterprise in development, the efficiency of market mechanisr
in the allocation of resources and the stimulation of productivi
under the proper management of the government is evident.
Whether or not the trade-off between productivity and distributive equity proves to be damaging to Pakistan involves a value
judgment and will be determined in the future. What becomes
economically significant is that Pakistan has been able to over
come monumental physical handicaps by adopting evolutionary
approaches and outward-looking economic policies.

In Burma, on the other hand, the lesson of development
confirms that not all government actions are efficient and that
a simple substitution of government for private enterprise can
be economically disastrous. In waging a relentless war agains
the phantom of the bourgeois, the military junta has drasticall
transformed economic organization on a magnificent scale--
with the net result of a stagnating economy, unprecedented in
the entire economic history of Burma. The fact that the command economy of Burma is only a caricature of those centrally
planned economies found in the Communist world in no way
prevents us from exhibiting it as a scare picture of economic
chaos, directly caused by the choice of inappropriate economic
policies.

In contemporary theorizing on economic development, an
argument seems to be prevalent that stresses the need for
large-scale state intervention, control and planning in the
light of the shortage of resources. The Burmese Way to Socia
ism endorsed this argument, proclaiming that, in the light of

the Marxian stage theory of economic development, Burma, historically, had slept under the shadow of feudalism, while capitalism was in full bloom in the Western world.[1] Indeed, the difference in initial conditions between the LDCs of Asia today and the Western countries in their early stages of economic development might have made "the challenge of state economic planning all the more dramatic."[2] Equally dramatic has been the frustration at failures in planning, socializing and controlling the economy, which are reminiscent of historical experiences in many developed countries that have traveled similar paths of modernization.

The precise problem of development by means of large-scale state actions has been an inability to coordinate and implement plans and policies on the national level, as well as the inequalities and rigidities of an LDC, including the state itself. At least, the Burmese experiment with a command economy testifies to the fact that a substitution of state for private economic actions in the name of removing inequalities and promoting growth can be more disastrous than tolerating certain inequities and market mechanisms.

Despite this historical unfairness, it should be remembered that the dramatic economic recovery of West Germany after the 1948 currency reform and the New Economic Policy era of the Soviet Union stand out as examples of a switch in economic policy from large-scale state intervention and control to decontrol, with the result of a relatively more efficient performance of the economy.[3] The same has been observed to be true of Pakistan in the 1950s and 1960s, where the dismantling of state controls improved economic performance by such leaps and bounds that G. Papanek termed it "confounding the prophets." There are many other examples within the region of Southeast Asia where the relative economic performance of outward-looking countries with a market-oriented economy has been far better than that of inward-looking countries with a heavily state-oriented economy. Indeed, the development pattern of LDCs today is not likely to be the same as that of developed countries in the early stages of modernization;[4] yet, the consequences of certain economic policies pursued by these countries are not without historical precedent. The Burmese case is, no doubt, unique to the sociopolitical and economic environment of Burma, though its recent experiences with evolutionary and revolutionary socialism have their counterparts in the history of economic development of many developed countries.

The Revolutionary Council's experiment with a command

economy in Burma is reminiscent of the experiences of Russia
in the years immediately following the Bolshevik Revolution.
The naivete of the new Russian rulers about the complexities
of constructing, managing and running an economy, the hostili
of educated civil servants and experts[5] to the new regime and
the disincentive effect of collectivization and socialization all
seem to be operating in different forms on the Burmese scene
The difference, of course, is that the Russian revolutionary
leaders had no historical lessons or stock of knowledge to rely
upon in the construction of a centrally planned economy, where
as the Revolutionary Council Government of Burma had at its
disposal a large stock of knowledge accumulated by the Communist world. Neither historical lessons, however, nor the
guidelines for appropriate economic actions embodied in that
knowledge, seem to have benefited the Revolutionary Council
greatly; and the resulting lack of historical perspective and
pragmatism on the part of Burmese policy-makers has been
responsible for the choice of inappropriate economic policies.
It is in this sense that the Burmese Way to Socialism is truly
unique and Burmese.

The failures of experimenting with a command economy
in Burma are due to a combination of factors, of which the
inability to control the loopholes attending a system of direct
controls seems most conspicuous. Policies of outright nationalization and rationing, without any effective machinery for
planning and control, have created an economic chaos of inefficiency and waste and are, therefore, wholly inappropriate,
in view of the factor endowment and economic arrangements
at the time of the military take over.

For one thing, there was no sign of abject poverty due to
a pernicious economic system of capitalism. The socialist
economy of the Pyidawtha Government might have been a fake
one in terms of the Burmese Way to Socialism, but it did not
tolerate or enhance the growth of industrial or financial capita
ism enabling one to endorse the poverty thesis of revolutionary
socialism. For another, there was no glaring inequity in income distribution comparable to pre-Communist Russia or
China to support a policy of outright nationalization and con-
fiscation of property and wealth from the landed aristocracy
or the bourgeois. The only pomeschiki or latifundia that
existed in independent Burma before 1962 was the state, which
was proclaimed to be the owner of all land and natural resourc
from 1948 on. In view of these economic arrangements and th
Burmese factor endowment, the economic policy of nationalization for equalization of incomes is neither necessary nor
appropriate.

The social structure and cultural system of Burma, also, do not seem to provide a viable framework for the functioning of a command economy. In the absence of rigidities with respect to social mobility and class distinctions in the traditional social system of Burma, the ideology of revolutionary socialism does not arouse either the national interest or active participation of the masses in the sociopolitical and economic programs of the Revolutionary Council. In a cultural system that lacks a strong concept of collectivity and social organization, coordinated planning and policies of development are difficult to concretize. Although the image of development envisioned in the Burmese Way to Socialism is group-focused, [6] the real process of implementing the goals of a socialist economy has been highly disorganized and haphazard, reflecting both Burmese personality and behavior. This lack of social discipline in planning and organization is a function of the deeply rooted value system embodied in Burmese Buddhism and the historical experience of individualism; it is evident in the process of decision-making and of managing the economy by a series of ad hoc councils, committees and boards with little or no coordination. The lack of any significant long-run economic plan and of any effective machinery for planning in the construction of a centrally planned economy further validates this cultural trait. Thus, significant cultural adaptation to a command economy seems to be absent among both the ruling military elite and the masses.

The People's Stores, operated under a system of rationing and price control, reveal the most glaring inefficiency of military management. Without any coordinated network of decision-making and control, the simple substitution of the military for the civilian entrepreneurial function has led to the development of a nationwide black market, with hyperinflation; the inability to administer a highly complex system of global quotas in the distribution of goods has resulted in the distortion of relative prices and an unorganized private black market of exchange among consumer goods. This problem of optimizing trade in products[7] was never pondered or planned in the Revolutionary Council scheme of rationing. As a result, the benevolent socialist goal of raising real income, as well as the equitable distribution of real income between citizens, has been defeated under mounting pressures of price inflation and contrived scarcity of goods.

The problem of maximizing production[8] was also ignored and relegated under the political facade of equity by launching liberal credit programs and peasant seminars without an

efficient system of allocation of resources to various uses or
effective supervision and control of production. The supposed
novel system of advance purchase of paddy introduced by the
Revolutionary Council is a case in point: the fixed low-price
policy, adopted in the name of equity, has not stimulated eithe
productivity or incentives, except for profits accruing to the
government from the price differential between the low interna
prices and high export prices of paddy. In an effort to cater t
the Burmese peasants, large loans have been poured into the
agricultural sector of the economy, with the net effect of a
continuous decline in agricultural yields and export. One perhaps may conclude that the agricultural programs of the Revolutionary Council have improved the cultivator's lot in terms c
income distribution, although depressed productivity and sky-
rocketing prices constitute a lower standard of living for the
people as a whole. The most pronounced effect of liberal
credit programs in the agricultural sector has been the disincentive effect, which is clearly revealed in the increasing
arrears of government loans.

Of all the requirements of a command economy, the one
that the military elite and also the Burmese social system has
most failed to meet is in matters of financial planning and
control. This is an aspect of cultural inadequacy, which may
be traced to the traditional value system, social and economic
environments of relative affluence and the cultural motivation
of the Burmese in general. The lack of a strong tradition of
parsimony and hard work, plus the stringent demand of financi
sophistication in a centralized system of banking, has been
responsible for the failures in nationalizing banks and in the
demonetization of K. 100 and K. 50 notes. In addition, there
has not been any significant program of currency reform or of
stabilizing the monetary system comparable to the Gosbank in
Russia or the Peoples Bank of China. As a conversion measur
with a capital levy on cash assets, the exchange of notes with
smaller denominations for K. 100 and K. 50 notes is unique in
the history of monetary reforms in both the Western and Sino-
Soviet worlds.[9] It is also unique with respect to its dramatic
failures in controlling inflation and subduing capitalists.

In the light of these experiences, it may be concluded that
the prerequisites for a centrally planned economy for Burma
are far more complex and demanding than a market-oriented
planned economy of evolutionary socialism. Burmese experience with a command economy also indicates the harsh reality
of an LDC's inability to meet the dramatic challenge of state
economic planning and control. The shortage of resources,

human and nonhuman, includes not only entrepreneurial talents
and the private flow of innovation but also planners and the
planning capacity of the state itself. The argument that large-
scale state intervention and control are indispensable to rapid
economic development[10] seems to ignore the possibility that
they can also be repressive in terms of development. In a
system of direct ownership and control of resources, there
is no such thing as an optimal amount of control that can stop
the need for incremental control in order to check the multiple
evasion of state actions. Indeed, the cycle of control-evasion-
control is among the so-called interlocking vicious circles of
poverty.

That economic therapies based upon the model of advanced
countries cannot be applied to the problems of LDCs is true not
only of transplanting modern capitalism but also of adopting a
centrally planned economy of the Sino-Soviet type. In order
to encompass an endless range of human activities and social
goals, the process of economic development in LDCs undoubtedly involves more than capital formation and maximization
of output. There is nothing wrong, therefore, in recognizing
economic development as a human problem,[11] but the excessive
preoccupation with doctrinal justification of ideal human conditions, which is characteristic of the Revolutionary Council
of Burma, can be economically disastrous. In short, experience in Burma shows that ideals of equity and justice in a
socialist society have very little meaning for the development
process in a real world of national poverty.

To be fair, it must be remembered that there are some
social benefits under the economic programs of the Burmese
Way to Socialism. Most of these relate to psychic income and
the emotional pride of the nationalist Burmese leadership. The
concept of national identity, which seems to occupy the highest
priority in the Burmese attitude toward development, has been
vigorously attained by the policy of societal insulation; and although it is doubtful whether or not the traditional cultural
integrity of Burma has been preserved through the socialist
programs of the Revolutionary Council Government, a sense
of national pride in being able to reject Western influence and
aid has been accomplished. This negative sovereignty and
nationalism, so abundantly asserted, has given great satisfaction to both the ruling military elite and the masses. Discrimination against aliens, including those trained and educated
in the West, might have been economically undesirable in increasing the need for human resources such as entrepreneural
talents; yet fulfillment of their roles by traditionally oriented

individuals and social groups offers a wider socioeconomic
horizon. Last but not the least, the policy of societal insulatic
and political neutralism in international relations seem to have
spared Burma from being drawn into the Cold War.

These benefits, set against the economic disaster of the
1960s, look gloomy for Burma's future development. If the
most crucial concern of LDCs such as Burma and Pakistan is
the preservation of national and cultural integrity, Burma's
policy certainly seems appropriate. It is my argument, however, that economic development is a prerequisite to this goal
and that modernization through resurrection of a glorious
traditional heritage is, at best, a dream. Thus from the experience of Burma and Pakistan, two basic conclusions on the
developmental process emerge: (a) measures of massive state
controls for the sake of traditional cultural integrity can retar
economic development and (b) an evolutionary approach via
outward-looking development policy can be more effective than
a revolutionary approach embodying drastic changes in socioeconomic organization.

A set of corollary conclusions may be drawn concerning
the relative economic performance and strategy of developmen
in Burma and Pakistan. First, the case of Pakistan seems to
demonstrate rigorously that the cause of economic underdevelc
ment does not necessarily lie in the shortage of innate factor-
endowments and of physical resources, in particular; the case
of Burma supports this conclusion and indicates the importanc
of traditional cultural obstacles to development. Second,
Pakistan is a more open society toward the West, both historically and culturally, which accounts for its more pragmatic
and modern outlook toward social change and economic develop
ment. Although the socioeconomic structures of the two countries do not seem to fit the patterns of development policy and
goals adopted, the types of social conflict and change have
produced different degrees of receptivity to the inflow of advanced technology, value systems and capital. In this sense,
Pakistan's cultural capital may be deemed as greater than that
of Burma. Third, the social structure and the role of religion
cannot be taken as static parameters of development policy anc
goals. The basic dilemma for Burma lies in the question of
the economic price that must be paid for the insulation of
society in the name of "isms," while Pakistan's critical dilem
ma lies in the political and cultural price that must be paid in
order to open the social system to various external sources of
technology and capital.

From these conclusions, two basic policy implications ma

be interpolated: (a) the importance of establishing an open
society to absorb advanced alien technology, capital and value
systems and (b) the importance of establishing an open economy
within the framework of the existing international economy. In
view of the tremendous societal bias and political nationalism
pervading the mentality of the goal-achieving political elite in
many LDCs, these objectives seem politically unattainable.
Yet the realities of development dictate that simple imitation
of advanced forms of economic systems and large-scale state
controls rarely elevate the state of technology or automatically
promote development. The process of economic development
is ipso facto an aspect of the social propensity to adapt and
innovate advanced methods of production and organization
appropriate to the sociopolitical structure of a country. Policy
suggested by an open social system must not be taken as a sacrifice of national and cultural identity; it is, rather, a means
of widening socioeconomic horizons on the societal level via
contact and conflict-resolution between modernity and traditionalism, the accumulation of cultural capital and the acceptance of the cultural price that must be paid to modernize. In
the same way, policy suggested by an open economy must not
be taken as free trade or laissez-faire in the traditional sense
but as pragmatic programs and measures of participation in
the existing international economy, along with maximum util-
ization of external capital. A strategy of development based
upon these guidelines may produce "balanced growth" between
social change and economic development, between domestic
and external sectors of the economy and, most important, between sociopolitical and economic goals.

                              NOTES

    1. Party Seminar 1965 . . ., p. 28.

    2. Myrdal, Asian Drama, op. cit., p. 715.

    3. See Henry C. Wallich, Mainsprings of the German
Revival (New Haven, Conn.: Yale University Press, 1955),
pp. 13-14; also, Mikhail V. Condoide, The Soviet Financial
System: Its Development and Relations with the Western
World (Columbus: Ohio State University, 1951), p. 25.

    4. Myrdal, op. cit., p. 712.

5.   Condoide, op. cit., p. 24.

6.   See A. O. Hirschman, The Strategy of Economic Development (New Haven, Conn.: Yale University Press, 1959), p. 486.

7.   J. E. Meade, The Stationery Economy (London: G. Allen and Unwin, 1965), p. 200.

8.   Ibid.

9.   See Leland B. Yeager, International Monetary Relations: Theory, History and Policy (New York: Harper & Row, 1966), pp. 345-46.

10.   Myrdal, op. cit.

11.   Ibid., p. 711.

ABOUT THE AUTHOR

Mya Maung, Associate Professor on the faculty of the School of Management at Boston College, has done extensive research into the problems of the developing Asian countries. In 1961, he served as Research Director on a project studying agricultural cooperation in Burma, which was conducted under the auspices of the Asia Foundation and the Government of the Union of Burma. For the past two years, Professor Maung has been involved in research as a consultant in International Development Studies at the Fletcher School of Law and Diplomacy, Tufts University.

Before coming to Boston College in 1966, Dr. Maung was on the faculty of the Department of Economics at South Dakota State University. Two years prior to that, he served as Assistant Professor of economics at Kansas State Teachers College. Before returning to the United States in 1963, Dr. Maung spent a year as Head of the Economics Department in the Defense Services Academy, Maymyo, Burma.

Professor Maung studied economics at the University of Rangoon, Burma; the Massachusetts Institute of Technology; the University of Michigan; and the Catholic University of America, Washington, D. C., from which he received his Ph. D. degree in 1961.

RENEWALS 458-4574
DATE DUE

NOV 2 1			
DEC 1 1			

GAYLORD

PRINTED IN U.S.A.